THE
WRITING
ON THE
WALL

MIKE READ

THE WRITING ON THE WALL

100 Iconic Blue Plaques
Commemorating
Britain's History

UNICORN

Published in 2018 by
Unicorn, an imprint of Unicorn Publishing Group LLP
101 Wardour Street
London
W1F 0UG
www.unicornpublishing.org

ISBN 978-1-911604266

Illustrated by Felicity Price-Smith
Designed by Barnaby Neale

———————◆———————

This book is dedicated to all the men and women, from all walks of life, who have enriched and contributed to our country and its history.

Their footprint from the past is recognised in the present and will hopefully inspire others in the future.

———————◆———————

FOREWORD

———————◆———————

This is a noble and endlessly fascinating cause.

For me, history is about people-watching. Looking at those
who made a mark on the past is particularly rewarding,
because that is how we learn so much through their triumphs
and disappointments. They are a benchmark against which
we can measure an age, as well as our own era.

There are few things that add to a journey more than spotting
a blue plaque, and having my memory jogged about a
noteworthy figure from the past. Political and military greats
are of course commemorated with statues across the land.
But more intriguing are the plaques dedicated to artists,
musicians and social innovators whose roll-call gives a clue to
what Britain is all about.

Mike Read loves this country, and he loves the past. This
book brings together his twin passions in a cleverly crafted
way. He avoids jingoistic nonsense, while celebrating
individual brilliance and quirkiness – things that England has
provided in abundance.

- Charles, 9th Earl Spencer

———————◆———————

CONTENTS

CONTENTS

INTRODUCTION

It was William Ewart, MP and pioneer of free libraries, who first came up with the notion of commemorating the homes of celebrated people with historical markers. The idea was taken up by the Society of Arts, which later became the Royal Society of Arts. How wonderful, then, that his own name appears on a blue plaque, albeit for his work on public libraries and not for suggesting the commemorative plaque scheme.

The first blue plaque was erected to Lord Byron in 1867, but the house (in Holles Street) was later demolished, leaving the oldest existing plaque as the one commemorating Napoleon III in King Street, St James's, Westminster, which was put up later that same year.

In 1901, the newly-formed London County Council took over the responsibility for the scheme, which remained under the municipal umbrella until the demise of the Greater London Council in 1986. It then passed to English Heritage, the scheme still focusing, as it always had, on London.

A blue plaque is a recognised symbol of our national heritage, a living footprint of our history, and serves as a permanent reminder of important contributions to the history of the country, commemorating notable, influential, and successful people from all walks of life.

English Heritage is a fantastic organisation, continuing to concentrate solely on the capital when it comes to blue plaques. As there are many worthy recipients across the whole of the country, and technology has led to an increased demand for more immediate recognition, other organisations have answered the call to arms. As well as several local schemes, national organisations such as The British Plaque Trust and the Heritage Foundation have installed blue plaques across the nation over the last twenty-five years.

My publisher suggested that I simply start with a current plaque and then link, by whatever means, to the next; I enjoy a challenge. Of course, it would be easy to remain in the same genre as there are easier and more obvious connections, so I have tried to go for unusual or unlikely links where possible.

 Look for the little link icon that illustrates the logical step between one entry and the next.

In 2017, for BBC Music Day, almost fifty plaques were erected in conjunction with the British Plaque Trust to commemorate our musical heritage across all genres, including pop, rock, folk, jazz, classical, and opera. Only one artist featured on three plaques - David Bowie. A very good place to start.

DAVID BOWIE

Bowie songs such as *Starman, Suffragette City, Moonage Daydream, All the Young Dudes* and *The Jean Genie* were all published by Titanic Music and recorded at Trident Studios, St Anne's Court, Soho. The plaque erected there in June 2017 by the BBC and the British Plaque Trust already features on guided tours. Another plaque that features Bowie went up on Hull railway station, the terminus being the start point for Bowie's backing group The Spiders from Mars.

Bowie is also commemorated in Maidstone, where he was part of the group the Mannish Boys during 1964 and 1965. He was still David Jones then, and lived some of the time in a van in London's Denmark Street to be close to where the action was. Denmark Street was known as Tin Pan Alley, which is also featured in this book, and now has its own blue plaque. In the 1960s, the street was home to most of the UK's best-known and most successful publishers, so there was no more logical or ideal place to hang out if you were an aspiring songwriter.

He was determined to be a star, and as well as his stint with the Mannish Boys, he tried name changes such as Davy Jones, David Jones & the Lower Third, and David Bowie & the Buzz, even releasing the comedy song *The Laughing Gnome*, and an album very much in the vocal style of Anthony Newley.

It wasn't until he was put together with producer Tony Visconti (in Tin Pan Alley) that things started to happen. Space Oddity launched a career that saw Bowie have hits from the late 1960s through to the late 2000s, including six studio albums, 10 live albums, 51 compilation albums and 128 singles, including five UK number ones.

He topped the singles chart with *Space Oddity*, *Ashes to Ashes*, *Under Pressure* (with Queen), *Let's Dance*, and *Dancing in the Street* (with Mick Jagger). His bestselling albums included *Hunky Dory*, *Aladdin Sane*, *Pin Ups*, *Diamond Dogs*, *The Rise and Fall of Ziggy Stardust*, and *Young Americans*.

Success would last until, and beyond, his untimely death in 2016. In 2017, the unsigned, hand-written lyrics to Starman sold at auction for over $81,000.

As well as several of Bowie's early songs being published by Titanic, Bowie's father, Haywood 'John' Stenton Jones, was a promotions officer for Dr. Barnardo's, (another blue plaque recipient featured in this book) and was born in 1912, the same year that the Titanic sank.

EDWARD SMITH

The *Titanic*'s captain, Edward John Smith, was an officer in the British Merchant Navy who joined the White Star Line in 1880, and later commanded several of their ships, including the *Baltic*, *Adriatic*, and *Olympic*. He was given command of the *Titanic*, which left Belfast for Southampton on 2nd April 1912, where she spent six days being prepared for her maiden voyage.

Captain Smith arrived on board at 7.30am on the day of departure, with a brief lifeboat drill taking place half an hour later. The first leg was the 84 miles to Cherbourg, where 22 unwittingly lucky passengers disembarked. 274 less fortunate boarded. At Queenstown, seven more disembarked and would probably talk about their good fortune for the rest of their lives. Another 120 boarded. It was scheduled as a return trip, with the journey back including a stop at Plymouth. There was no return trip.

The *Titanic* was four days into her crossing, on 15th April, when she struck an iceberg and sank, with the loss of over 1,500 lives. Smith himself went down with the ship. He was last heard shouting through a megaphone, 'Well boys, do your best for the women and children and look out for yourselves.' The last sighting of him was as a lone figure on the bridge. He was seen for many years as the epitome of the British stiff upper lip.

There is an unusually-styled plaque dedicated to Smith at his birthplace, 51, Well Street, Hanley, and a statue was erected to commemorate him in Beacon Park, Lichfield, in 1914. Ninety-eight years later, in 2012, a blue plaque was unveiled at 17, Marine Crescent, Sefton, Liverpool, where he lived from 1898 to 1907.

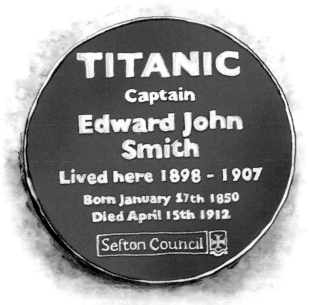

The British have always been a nation for not letting the side down, for rules, codifying and captaining, especially in the sporting arena. This is epitomised by Sir Henry Newbolt's **Vitai Lampada***:*
'But his captain's hand on his shoulder smote,
'Play up! Play up! And play the game.'
Apt then, that we move from a captain of one sort to another.

LEN HUTTON

We have always placed great importance on captains. If it goes wrong, as it did for Captain Smith, questions are asked and fingers point. If all goes well, there are accolades and rewards.

Sir Len Hutton, who skippered the England test team from 1952 to 1955, shares a blue plaque with fellow England batsman Herbert Sutcliffe, 1894-1978, with whom Hutton first appeared at the crease for Yorkshire in 1935, at the age of eighteen.

The senior had coached him in his garden while Hutton was still playing for his school. They both appeared in the same Yorkshire XI during the second half of the 1930s, Sutcliffe nearing the end of his career, and Hutton at the dawn of his. Len Hutton would captain the England test team from 1952 to 1955.

Hutton also has another plaque on his birthplace at Fulneck, Pudsey, near Leeds. Hutton played in 79 test matches between 1935 and 1955 and scored 364 runs against Australia in only his sixth test appearance, which remains an England test record.

He became the first professional 20th century cricketer to captain England in test matches, and is still regarded as one of the greatest batsmen in the history of the game.

The plaque unveiled by Len Hutton's sons, John and Richard, in 1916 at Pudsey St Lawrence Cricket Ground, where both Hutton and Sutcliffe began their careers.

◆————————

The bat used by Hutton on 27th December 1948, when he scored the world record opening partnership of 359 with Cyril Washbrook at Johannesburg, is in the MCC museum at Lord's Cricket Ground.

The site of Lord's Cricket Ground 1811-1813 itself displays a blue plaque that celebrates the history of the ground, with Hutton and many others contributory players in the iconic status of the current ground.

Hutton notched up 812 runs at Lord's in just twelve matches, his highest score being 196.

LORD'S CRICKET GROUND

Lord's Cricket ground was initially created on Dorset Fields, now Dorset Square, and was founded by Thomas Lord who has a plaque in his honour at his birthplace in Thirsk.

The first match played there was in 1787 and the Marylebone Cricket Club (MCC) set down the Code of Laws of the game. The first Eton v Harrow match was also played there, in 1805. This is now referred to as 'Lord's Old Ground'.

In 1809, with London expanding rapidly and rents rising, Lord dug up the turf and relocated to a second cricket ground in Eyre's Estate, St. John's Wood, the Dorset Fields site yielding to the inevitable just two years later.

The second ground proved to be unpopular and lacking in atmosphere, but this time London's development was on Lord's side. The new Regent's Canal was scheduled to cut right through the outfield of his new ground, so with £4,000 compensation he took another site, also on the Eyre Estate, which he'd been offered. Again, Lord removed the turf and re-laid it a few hundred yards to the north-west.

The earliest known match on the new pitch was between the MCC and Hertfordshire on 22nd June 1814, and the ground continues to be hallowed turf for cricket fans around the world.

Not surprisingly, with so many English settlers, cricket was played in British North America from the 1700s and by the time of the US Civil War was vying with baseball for popularity. As baseball grew, cricket declined.

Although Buddy Holly's group were named after the insect and not the sport, when Buddy Holly & the Crickets flew in to London in late February 1958 for what would be their only UK tour, their English record label knew the ideal PR story for the media. The group was driven to Whisky A Go Go for The Crickets to be photographed being taught to play cricket by Len Hutton's team-mates, England batsman, Denis Compton (who has a stand named after him at Lords), and England wicket-keeper, Godfrey Evans.

It was all good PR, and for a new young American star to be linked with two of Britain's greatest sportsmen was no bad thing.

BUDDY HOLLY
& THE CRICKETS

Charles Hardin Holley was born on September 7, 1936, in Lubbock, Texas. He acquired his nickname from his mother, who thought that 'Buddy' was far more of a fitting name for her little boy. His surname was misspelled on his first recording contract, and the stage name 'Buddy Holly' stuck.

He was musically talented from a very early age and became a regular perfomer during his teens. On February 13th 1955, Buddy Holly appeared as half of the duo Buddy & Bob, at the bottom of a bill at Lubbock, Texas, Fairpark Coliseum. Top of the bill was Elvis Presley, who lent Buddy his Martin guitar. Holly opened twice more that year for Elvis at the same venue.

It is not an exaggeration to say that Elvis was a huge influence on the young Holly, and his bandmates (later to become known as The Crickets) testified to the role that Elvis' music played in shaping Holly's sound. However,

Holly would become a hugely influential performer and songwriter in his own right, and one who helped shape the sound of modern popular music. He wrote commerical hits that are still played to this day, such as his breakthrough hit *That'll be the Day* (inspired by a line in the John Wayne film *The Searchers*) in 1957, and *Peggy Sue*. The Beatles named themselves as an echo of The Crickets, and Holly inspired fledgling talents such as the 17-year-old Bob Dylan, who saw what was to be Buddy's final tour in 1958. The Rolling Stones were also to score their first chart hit with a cover of Buddy Holly's *Not Fade Away* in 1964.

It was during this tour that Buddy Holly took the fateful flight which would tragically claim his life, at just 22 years of age, when his plane crashed shortly after it left the ground. Also aboard were fellow Rock 'n' Roll acts Richie Valens and The Big Bopper. There were no survivors.

*Buddy Holly's musical hero and chief influence Elvis Presley recorded the song **Harbour Lights** during his first commercial recording session at Sun Studios for Sam Phillips on July 5th 1954, and it was his first ever first track to go on tape. The song was written by Jimmy Kennedy.*

JIMMY KENNEDY

Jimmy Kennedy got the idea for the song *Harbour Lights* after taking a wrong turning en route from Southampton to Weybridge and finding himself in the car park of an inn called the Harbour Lights at Cosham, near Portsmouth.

First sung by Frances Langford, it became the UK's bestselling song of 1937, being recorded by numerous big bands of the day including Ambrose and his Orchestra. The song became popular all over again in 1950 when Guy Lombardo's version climbed to No. 2 with six other versions also selling well, including a rendition by Bing Crosby and Vera Lynn, who recorded it more than once.

Ten years later, *Harbour Lights* got a third bite of the cherry when The Platters had a big hit with it. Other artists who have recorded the song include Rudy Vallee, Pat Boone, Sammy Kaye, Ray Anthony, Clyde McPhatter, The Ink Spots, Bing Crosby, Jerry Lee Lewis, and Engelbert Humperdinck.

Kennedy was the most successful British songwriter in the US, until Lennon and McCartney, as well as having an amazing run in the UK. Kennedy wrote or co-wrote such classics as *The Hokey Cokey, Teddy Bears' Picnic, Lili Marlene, Red Sails in the Sunset, South of the Border, My Prayer, Istanbul (Not Constantinople), The Isle of Capri, We're Going to Hang Out the Washing (On the Siegfried Line)* and *Love Is Like a Violin*.

The blue plaque for Jimmy Kennedy and Harbour Lights was erected at the hostelry as part of BBC Music Day in 2017 and unveiled by his son Jimmy. The song remains one of the most requested in America. It's also something pretty special for a writer when Elvis Presley's first ever recording is not only your creation, but was also inspired by a British pub.

BBC Music Day

JIMMY KENNEDY

songwriter

1902-1984

The idea for the song Harbour Lights came to him here in 1937. The song has been recorded by Elvis Presley, Bing Crosby, The Platters and over 100 other artists.

Awarded by BBC Radio Solent

British Plaque Trust

When Elvis made his first ever appearance on CBS's Ed Sullivan Show in the States, on September 9th 1956, he pulled in viewing figures of 72 million. The host, unusually, wasn't Ed Sullivan, who was recuperating after a car accident, but English actor Charles Laughton who deputised for a couple of weeks.

CHARLES LAUGHTON

Charles Laughton, born in Yorkshire in 1899 to a wealthy family of hoteliers, has his blue plaque at 15, Percy Street, Camden. Laughton, who trained at RADA, first took to the stage professionally in the mid 1920s, going on to play Shakespearean roles at the Old Vic before heading to Broadway and then Hollywood. Daniel Day-Lewis regards Laughton as one of his inspirations: 'He was probably the greatest film actor who came from that period of time. He had something quite remarkable. His generosity as an actor, he fed himself into that work. As an actor, you cannot take your eyes off him.'

Among Laughton's major films were *The Barretts of Wimpole Street*, *Jamaica Inn*, *The Hunchback of Notre Dame*, and *The Private Life of Henry VIII*, in which he starred with his wife, Elsa Lanchester. He won an Oscar as Best Actor for his portrayal of the Tudor king, the movie also winning an Oscar for Best Picture.

*In the 1935 film **Mutiny on the Bounty**, Clark Gable played Fletcher Christian and Charles Laughton was Captain Bligh. Bligh has his own plaque a few miles across London from Laughton's, in Lambeth.*

CAPTAIN WILLIAM BLIGH

Bligh's plaque at 100, Lambeth Road is opposite the Imperial War Museum, and was erected to commemorate the 180th anniversary of his sailing with *The Bounty* in 1787 and the subsequent mutiny. On 28th April 1789, about half of the crew mutinied, under the command of acting Lieutenant Fletcher Christian, setting Bligh and eighteen who remained loyal to him adrift in a 23ft launch.

They were given food and water for a week, four cutlasses, a quadrant, and a compass. Incredibly, he covered 3,600 miles in just 48 days, landing at the South-East Asian island of Timor, on June 12th and making it back to England the following March. Bligh was acquitted of losing his ship, and by the time he retired he had been promoted to the rank of Admiral.

 The explorer Ernest Shackleton is another British sea captain who has been commemorated with a blue plaque.

SIR ERNEST SHACKLETON

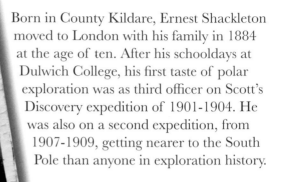

Born in County Kildare, Ernest Shackleton moved to London with his family in 1884 at the age of ten. After his schooldays at Dulwich College, his first taste of polar exploration was as third officer on Scott's Discovery expedition of 1901-1904. He was also on a second expedition, from 1907-1909, getting nearer to the South Pole than anyone in exploration history.

In 1908, he'd attempted his own South Pole expedition, named Nimrod, but his hopes of becoming the first person to reach the pole were dashed when he was forced to turn back early in 1909, with just 97 miles to go. Shackleton was knighted for his achievements by Edward VII, but after Amundsen won the race to the South Pole he looked at the becoming the first man to cross Antarctica from sea to sea via The Pole.

His Imperial Trans-Antarctic expedition came to a disastrous end with his ship, *The Endurance*, becoming trapped in pack ice, but he continued his exploits in the *James Caird*, named after a major sponsor, a jute manufacturer in Dundee. Shackleton died in 1922, in South Georgia on board the Quest whilst on the Shackleton-Rowett expedition and was buried there. In 1956, one of Shackleton's contemporaries said 'Scott for scientific method, Amundsen for speed and efficiency, but when disaster strikes and all hope is gone, get down on your knees and pray for Shackleton.'

In 1928, a blue plaque was erected at his former home by London County Council at 12 Westwood Hill, Sydenham, London.

Shackleton's final expedition was sponsored by an old school friend from Dulwich College, Dr. J.Q. Rowett, Rowett presenting the school with Shackleton's previous ship, the *James Caird*. It now resides in the establishment's North Cloister.

Shackleton's heroics have recently been popularised by films and television documentaries. In 2009, three of Shackleton's descendants, Henry Worsley, Will Gow and Henry Adams, completed the 900-mile journey to the South Pole, attempted by their ancestor in 1908/9. They referred to it as 'unfinished family business'.

Another former Dulwich College pupil to be recognised with a blue plaque or two is writer PG Wodehouse, who remained extremely proud of being an Old Alleynian, having edited the school magazine from 1899-1900 and played for the 1st XV and the 1st XI.

P. G. WODEHOUSE

Sir Pelham Grenville Wodehouse KBE, the son of a Hong Kong-based magistrate, Wodehouse has a clutch of plaques. A brown plaque at 1, Vale Place, Guildford, Surrey commemorates his birthplace which, due to road redevelopment, is on the wall of 59, Epsom Road. A blue plaque was unveiled in 1988 by HM Queen Elizabeth, the Queen Mother at 17, Dunraven Street, London, WI, which was called Norfolk Street when Wodehouse and his wife Leonora lived there. Her Majesty made a short speech at the ceremony in praise of the creator of the inimitable Bertie Wooster and his manservant Jeeves:

'I am particularly pleased to have been invited to unveil this plaque, as for many years I have been an ardent reader of P.G. Wodehouse. Indeed I am proud to say that his very first book, The Pothunters, was dedicated by him to members of my family… Sir Pelham Wodehouse succeeded in the great ambition of so many novelists. Not only has he brought new words and expressions into the English language, but he has also created characters whose names have become household words; Jeeves and Bertie, Lord Emsworth and his prize pig, the Empress of Blandings and even Aunt Agatha to name but a few, live on as immortal characters. His gift is that, fifty or sixty years after many of his books were written, they still make us laugh, and I am sure that generations to come will continue to laugh at them just as much as we have done. What an encouraging thought for the future.'

A plaque was also erected in 1996 at Threepwood, Record Road, Emsworth, where Wodehouse lived periodically between 1904 and 1914, and was unveiled by the actor Ian Carmichael. Carmichael portrayed Bertie Wooster in 20 episodes of the BBC series *The World of Wooster*, between 1965 and 1967, featuring Dennis Price as Jeeves and Derek Nimmo as Bingo Little.

A fourth plaque adorns, 'The Little Church Around the Corner,' the Church of Transfiguration in New York, where Pelham married Ethel Rowley Wayman at the end of September 1914. The plaque was sponsored by America's Wodehouse Society. There is another plaque at Walton Street, just behind Harrods. Many have questioned the 'L.L.A.D.' on the Walton Street plaque, which are actually the initials for a now archaic cockney expression, 'Lord love a duck,', which Wodehouse used in his books on several occasions. His earliest use of the phrase is in *The Coming of Bill*: '"Well, Lord love a duck!" replied the butler, who in his moments of relaxation was addicted to homely expletives of the lower London type.' Although Jeeves and Wooster were his most popular creations, he also had success with the garrulous Old Etonian, Psmith, with a silent 'P.' Wodehouse based the character on Rupert D'Oyley Carte, the son of the Gilbert and Sullivan impresario, Richard D'Oyley Carte, an acquaintance of his cousin's at Winchester College. The Blandings books, another Wodehouse creation, was also made into a TV series.

Wodehouse moved to France before WWII, was subsequently taken prisoner by the Nazis, and never returned to England, living out the rest of his long life in the United States, where he died in 1975 aged ninety-three.

Wodehouse took the name of Bertie Wooster's manservant, Jeeves, from cricketer Percy Jeeves, after watching him play for Goole CC. Wodehouse and his mentor, fellow plaque recipient mentioned in this tome, Arthur Conan Doyle, were both passionate about cricket.

PERCY JEEVES

Percy Jeeves was a first-class cricketer born in 1888, who played locally for Goole CC before turning professional with Hawes CC and being given a trial for Yorkshire. It was while Jeeves was playing for Hawes that P. G. Wodehouse saw him in action, during a summer holiday in Wensleydale.

Over 50 years later, Wodehouse explained: 'I suppose Jeeves' bowling must have impressed me, for I remembered him in 1916 when I was in New York and starting the Jeeves and Bertie saga, and it was just the name I wanted. I remember admiring his action, very much.'

In 1912, Percy Jeeves joined Warwickshire as a county player, proving himself to be a very solid batsman and bowler. In 1914 he played for the Players against the Gentlemen at the Oval, taking 4-44, with Plum Warner predicting a bright future for the young player.

With the outbreak of WWI, Jeeves joined the Royal Warwickshire Regiment and was killed eighteen months later in July 1916 at High Wood during the Battle of the Somme, just as Wodehouse was writing his surname into the history books.

 *High Wood is is alluded to in Siegfried Sassoon's poem **Died of Wounds**. Fellow poet Robert Graves survived grave wounds in that same battle.*

His wet white face and miserable eyes
Brought nurses to him more than groans and sighs:
But hoarse and low and rapid rose and fell
His troubled voice: he did the business well.

The ward grew dark; but he was still complaining
And calling out for 'Dickie'. 'Curse the Wood!
'It's time to go. O Christ, and what's the good?
'We'll never take it, and it's always raining.'

I wondered where he'd been; then heard him shout,
'They snipe like hell! O Dickie, don't go out...
I fell asleep ... Next morning he was dead;
And some Slight Wound lay smiling on the bed.

- Siegfried Sassoon

SIEGFRIED SASSOON

Born Siegfried Sassoon in 1886 in Kent, Sassoon was initially educated at New Beacon School, Sevenoaks, before going to Marlborough College and Clare College, Cambridge, where he read history. His family were wealthy but Siegfried's father was disinherited for marrying outside his faith, while his mother was one of the Thornycroft family, well-known for their skill as sculptors.

His parents, however, split up when he was just four years old. Along with other plaque recipients in this book, Nick Drake and Sir John Betjeman, Sassoon was a pupil at Marlborough College. He later attended Cambridge University, but left without ganing a degree.He existed on a small legacy, playing cricket, hunting and writing poetry, but an aunt later left him a substantial amount, with which he bought Heytesbury House in Wiltshire. His first literary success was *The Daffodil Murderer* in 1913. He was desperate to play first-class cricket for Kent, but was not deemed to be good enough. He did, however, play to a good standard, sometimes alongside fellow future plaque recipient Arthur Conan Doyle.

Sassoon's enthusiasm for the game remained undiminished and he continued to play the game into his seventies. His patriotism saw him joining the Sussex Yeomanry before the outbreak of WWI. After a period of convalescence due to a broken arm, he was commissioned into the 3rd Battalion of the Royal Welch Fusiliers and was sent to France where he met and became friends with fellow poet Robert Graves. Sassoon's suicidal missions, such as capturing trenches single-handed, bringing in the wounded under heavy fire, and scattering the enemy with grenades, earned him the nickname of 'Mad Jack,' and saw him being awarded the Military Cross.

Despite being decorated for his bravery on the Western Front, his horror of what he saw as a jingoistic war and the death of his close friend David Cuthbert Thomas, led him to protest against the continuation of the conflict in his *Soldier's Declaration* of 1917. He reasoned that he had joined a war of defence and liberation which had become one of aggression and conquest. Instead of being court-martialled, he was admitted to

Craiglockhart military psychiatric hospital, where he became friends with fellow poet Wilfred Owen.

Despite throwing his ribbon of his Military Cross into the River Mersey, Sassoon returned to active service, but while in France as acting captain he was wounded by friendly fire and spent the remainder of the war in Britain. He retained the rank of Captain.

After the war he continued to write, one of his most enduring works being the award-winning *Memoirs of a Fox-Hunting Man*. The follow up was *Memoirs of an Infantry Officer*. Sassoon is one of sixteen Great War poets commemorated in Poets' Corner at Westminster Abbey.

 Sassoon was formally introduced to fellow poet Rupert Brooke at a breakfast party at Eddie Marsh's rooms at Raymond Buildings, Grey's Inn.

RUPERT BROOKE

Following his sojourn in Canada, America, and Tahiti, any political, theatrical and literary plans were put on hold as the country went to war with Germany. Rupert Brooke joined up and saw action at Antwerp before being seconded to the Hood Battalion and setting sail from Bristol on the *SS Grantully Castle* for Gallipoli. Lying gravely ill with Septicaemia on a French hospital ship, he heard the Dean of St Pauls, Dean Inge, had read his poem *The Soldier* during a service at the cathedral, the poem's opening lines becoming two of the most famous lines of poetry in the English language:

'If I should die, think only this of me:
That there's some corner of a foreign field
That is forever England.'

Brooke died of Septicaemia one day short of the Gallipoli landings and is buried in an olive grove on the island of Skyros. Brooke's unrequited love was Noel Olivier, although he later had relationships with several women, including Elisabeth van Rysselberghe, Ka Cox, Lady Eileen Wellesley, actress Cathleen Nesbitt, and artist Phyllis Gardner.

The only liaison to produce a child was his affair with a lady called Taatamata in Tahiti. In 1915 she gave birth to his daughter, Arlice Rapoto. This has now been researched by genealogists and it seems that Arlice either died in the 1990s or in 2005 aged 90.

Brooke has a blue plaque on the house where he was born at 5, Hillmorton Road, Rugby, although he grew up at Rugby School where his father was a housemaster, until his death. The house to which his mother then moved also has plaque, the wording featuring them both.

A plaque to Brooke was unveiled at the Orchard, Grantchester in 2015 on the 100th anniversary of his death, by Dame Pippa Harris, the grand-daughter of Brooke's first love, Noel Olivier, her sister Tamsin, and William Pryor, the grandson of Brooke's close friends, Jacques and Gwen Raverat.

There is also a plaque at the family home in Rugby.

Rupert Brooke
Poet & Soldier 1887 - 1915
Lived and wrote at The Orchard
1909 - 1911, and at
The Old Vicarage 1911 - 1912

British Plaque Trust

The witness on Rupert Brooke's only publishing contract was Virginia Woolf.
Woolf and Rupert Brooke first met as children while holidaying with their
families at St Ives in Cornwall, rekindling their acquaintance some years later.

VIRGINIA WOOLF

As well as being part of the Bloomsbury Group, she and her husband, Leonard Woolf, founded their own publishing company, the Hogarth Press, at the house in Richmond, two years after her debut novel, *The Voyage Out*. Virginia wrote nine novels in all, including *Mrs Dalloway*, *To the Lighthouse*, and *Orlando*, as well as many short stories, biographies and non-fiction, including *A Room of One's Own*.

Initially home-educated whilst her older brothers were sent to Cambridge, Woolf had a voracious appetite for learning, later studying at the 'Ladies Department' at King's College, London. Despite her literary success, Woolf was dogged for much of her life by nervous breakdowns and mental problems, which she ascribed to her having been sexually abused by her half-brothers when she was a child, and the death of her mother when Woolf was just 13 years old. She writes about her early traumas frankly in the essays *A Sketch of the Past* and *22 Hyde Park Gate*.

Unable to overcome the deep depression which would regularly assail her, Woolf took her own life in 1941 at the age of fifty-nine, leaving this note for her husband:

'Dearest, I feel certain that I am going mad again. I feel we can't go through another of those terrible times. And I shan't recover this time. I begin to hear voices, and I can't concentrate. So I am doing what seems the best thing to do. You have given me the greatest possible happiness. You have been in every way all that anyone could be. I don't think two people could have been happier 'til this terrible disease came. I can't fight any longer. I know that I am spoiling your life, that without me you could work. And you will I know. You see I can't even write this properly. I can't read. What I want to say is I owe all the happiness of my life to you. You have been entirely patient with me and incredibly good. I want to say that — everybody knows it. If anybody could have saved me it would have been you. Everything has gone from me but the certainty of your goodness. I can't go on spoiling your life any longer. I don't think two people could have been happier than we have been. V.'

A blue plaque adorns her former home at Hyde Park Gate, Kensington.

---

*A passage in Virginia Woolf's book **A Room of One's Own** mentions the idea that if Shakespeare had had a sister, she wouldn't have had the same opportunities as her brother because she was a woman.*

*The Smiths turned Virginia Woolf's idea into the song **Shakespeare's Sister**, the picture sleeve featuring an image of actress Pat Phoenix, best known for her role as Elsie Tanner in the TV series **Coronation Street** and as the step-mother of Cherie, wife of former Prime Minister, Tony Blair. Written by Morrissey and Johnny Marr, the song reached no. 26 in the chart in 1985. The Smiths feature on a blue plaque for Strawberry Studios in Stockport. On 3 May 2007 a plaque was mounted on the front of 3 Waterloo Road by the Borough of Stockport for the Stockport Heritage Trust.*

STRAWBERRY STUDIOS

Strawberry was originally called Inter-City Studios and owned by
the former road manager for Billy J. Kramer and the Dakotas, Peter
Tattersall. He brought in Mindbenders guitarist Eric Stewart as a partner
and they moved the studio to No.3 Waterloo Road, Stewart re-naming it
after the Beatles classic *Strawberry Fields Forever.*

Their first hit to emerge from the studio was *Neanderthal Man*, by Hot Legs,
the musicians comprising Stewart, Graham Gouldman, Lol Creme and
Kevin Godley, who would become 10cc. Eric Stewart described it: 'It was
a very tiny studio with some stereo equipment and the walls lined with egg
boxes to provide sound insulation. There was a makeshift sort of control
desk tied together with Sellotape and string, but it was good enough for
what I wanted to do, and it was the only studio near Manchester.'

Graham Gouldman was also enthusiastic about the project: 'Ever since I'd
started songwriting I'd always wanted to have a studio of my own to work
in and to make my own demos. We used to tell ourselves that one day the
Beatles would record there – and eventually Paul McCartney did.'

It wasn't long before the studio got a name for itself because of the
commercial success of the recordings it was producing. From such humble
beginnings, a substantial and well-known enterprise was quite quickly
established. One of the studio's hits, *Umpopo* (recorded as Doctor Father)
attracted the attention of Neil Sedaka, who subsequently decided to
record two albums there, using the in-house musicians: *Solitaire* (1972) and
The Tra-La Days are Over (1973).

These albums were so succesful for Sedaka, that it made the musicians
who'd acted as his backing band think twice - why should they be working
for flat-rate studio fees when they could be recording their own material,
and making more money into the bargain?

And thus the band 10cc was born, recording their first four albums at Strawberry. They were hugely successful, as was the studio itself, and the studios expanded and played host to a number of varied and famous musical acts, some of whom are now commemorated on the blue plaque on the building which once housed the studio.

The studio closed its doors for the last time in 1993, but its place in the history of popular music is assured.

As well as featuring on the plaque for Strawberry Studios, alongside The Smiths, Paul McCartney is also featured on a plaque for the only appearances he and John Lennon made as a duo, when they called themselves The Nerk Twins.

JOHN LENNON & PAUL McCARTNEY

The Beatles had their first hit late in 1962, and the following year became the hottest act in the world, but back in the spring of 1960 a 19-year-old John Lennon and a 17-year-old Paul McCartney hitched with their guitars from Liverpool to Caversham in Berkshire.

Their destination? This pub, The Fox and Hounds, a short walk from Reading town centre.

Paul recalled, 'That spring of 1960, John and I went down to a pub in Reading, the Fox and Hounds, run by my cousin Betty Robbins and her husband Mike. We worked behind the bar. It was a lovely experience that came from John and I just hitching off down there. At the end of the week we played in the pub as the Nerk Twins. We even made our own posters.'

They presumably took the name from a character played by Harry Secombe in the radio series *The Goon Show*, Fred Nerk. John and Paul played twice over the weekend, their only gigs as a duo. They played acoustically and didn't even have microphones. Betty and her husband Mike, having previously been Butlin's Redcoats, had enough experience to give the duo a few tips. Most of the set, not surprisingly, was mainly rock and roll or country and western, but Mike looked at their setlist and spotted their version of Les Paul and Mary Ford's 1953 hit, *The World is Waiting for the Sunrise*.

Paul said, 'Betty's husband turned me on to showbusiness in a big way, and the talk we had with him about how we should do the show was very formative. He'd been an entertainment manager, hosting talent contests at Butlins and had been on the radio. He asked what we were going to open with and we said *Be Bop A Lula*. He told us "No good. You need to open with something fast and instrumental. This is a pub on a Saturday night. What else have you got?" We said, "Well, we do *The World is Waiting for the Sunrise*. I play the melody and John plays the rhythm." He said, "Perfect, start with that, then do *Be Bop a Lula*." He was good like that, and I would remember his advice years later when we were organising our shows.'

The Berkshire blue plaque commemorates the only appearance of the Nerk Twins and was unveiled by actress, comedian, singer/songwriter, and Paul McCartney's cousin, Kate Robbins. She was two years old and asleep in bed upstairs when John and Paul appeared at The Fox and Hounds.

BBC Music Day

JOHN LENNON &
PAUL McCARTNEY
played their only gig as
'The Nerk Twins'
at the Fox & Hounds
on 23rd April 1960

Awarded by
BBC Radio Berkshire

British Plaque Trust

*Paul McCartney wrote and recorded the theme for the James Bond movie **Live and Let Die**, which reunited him with Beatles producer George Martin, who arranged the orchestra break in the song. The single reached No. 2 in the US and No. 9 in the UK, earning McCartney an award in 2012 for 4 million plays in the States alone.*

IAN FLEMING

The debonnaire author and one-time real life wartime spy Ian Fleming is famed for creating the James Bond thrillers, which include *Casino Royale*, *From Russia With Love*, and *Goldfinger*.

President John F. Kennedy ensured that the 007 novels became popular after he named *From Russia With Love* as one of his favourite books. Fleming and Kennedy had met at a party at Washington DC, during which the author had made a humorous suggestion to the President as to how the US might rid itself of the threat from Fidel Castro, by claiming that beards attracted radioactivity. The idea was that Castro would shave off his beard, look like any ordinary man, and thus lose his power.

The amused JFK promised that he would at least read Fleming's books. His support helped catapult the books to becoming bestsellers.

 *Fleming lived at Ebury Street until 1945, when he purchased 15 acres on the north coast of Jamaica at Oracabessa Bay and built Goldeneye. In 1951, Fleming bought Noël Coward's house, White Cliffs, at St Margaret's in Kent; Fleming's sister-in-law, Celia Johnson, starred in Coward's films **In Which We Serve** and **Brief Encounter**.*

NOËL COWARD

Noël Peirce Coward, born in Teddington in 1899, was initially a juvenile actor, before becoming a successful playwright, director, songwriter, and singer, as well as continuing to act. His fifty plays include *Hay Fever*, *Blithe Spirit*, *Present Laughter*, and *Private Lives*. He won an Academy Honorary Award in 1943 for his film *In Which We Serve*. He became a favourite on US television in the 1950s, often performing his own songs such as *London Pride*, *Mud Dogs and Englishmen*, *Don't Put Your Daughter on the Stage Mrs. Worthington*, *A Room with a View*, and *I'll See You Again*.

Coward was knighted in 1969, four years before his death and burial at his house Firefly. In 1984, the Queen Mother, who had been a guest at this Jamaican hideaway, unveiled a memorial stone to him in Poets' Corner, in Westminster Abbey. She said: 'I came because he was my friend.' In 2006, the Albery Theatre in London was renamed the Noel Coward Theatre in his honour, and a seated statue of Coward, reclining nonchalantly with a cigarette, looks out over the sea from the garden at Firefly, just a few yards from his grave.

There are blue plaques commemorating 'The Master' at Teddington, Belgravia and Dymchurch.

 One of Coward's most famous and enduring songs was London Pride, written on Paddington railway station amidst the bomb damage of WWII.

PADDINGTON BEAR

Paddington first appeared in the autumn of 1958 in *A Bear Called Paddington*, the first of many books by Michael Bond. The tales of the bear who came from 'deepest, darkest Peru,' with his old suitcase, duffel coat and penchant for marmalade have been translated into some 30 languages and sold in the region of 30 million copies. Bizarrely, a Paddington Bear soft toy passed into the history books after being chosen by the British tunnellers to be the first item to be given to their French counterparts when the two sides were linked in 1994.

In the early 1960s, Michael Bond considered suing Shirlie and Eddie Clarkson who were selling Paddington toys without a licence. After an encounter in a lift, the three became friends, the Clarksons were given a licence and they made a small fortune from selling millions of Paddington Bears, even getting Bond to add the wellingtons in 1964 so the bear could stand up. Their young son, Jeremy, years before his time as *Top Gear* host, spent his youth surrounded by Paddington Bears.

Paddington's green plaque is fixed under the clock on Platform 1 at Paddington station.

PADDINGTON
BEAR

As described in Michael Bond's best-selling
book, 'A Bear Called Paddington', Paddington
Bear first arrived at Paddington Station
in 1958.

Scenes from his first big-screen adventure
'Paddington' were filmed here at the station
in the autumn of 2013.

Paddington is not the only bear to inspire a plaque; Rupert Bear's creator Mary Tourtel is commemorated in Canterbury.

MARY TOURTEL

Mary Tourtel was born Mary Caldwell at 52, Palace Street, Canterbury in 1874, the youngest daughter of a stained-glass artist and stonemason. She studied at the Sidney Cooper School of Art in Canterbury, went on to become an illustrator for children's books, and in 1900 married Hebert Bird Tourtel, Assistant Editor of the Daily Express.

In 1920, Herbert Tourtel, by then news editor of *The Express* was asked to produce a new comic strip to compete with *The Daily Mail*'s *Teddy Tail* and the *Daily Mirror*'s *Pip, Squeak and Wilfred*. Mary came up with *Little Lost Bear,* which was first published in 36 episodes in the paper on November 8th 1920, the early strips illustrated by Mary and captioned by Herbert. Initially having no name, the brown bear was changed to white to save costs on ink. In 1931, 1932, and 1933, *Monster Rupert* annuals were published that were much 'darker' than the later *Rupert* annuals, featuring ogres, ravens and crows. Herbert died in 1931 and Mary retired four years later after her health and eyesight deteriorated.

MARY TOURTEL
1874 - 1948
Creator of Rupert Bear
was born here
28 January 1874

*Punch illustrator Alfred Bestall took over writing and illustrating the **Rupert** strips. The first **Rupert** annual, illustrated by Bestall, appeared in 1936.*

ALFRED BESTALL

Alfred Edmeades Bestall took over *Rupert Bear* in the mid-1930s, writing and illustrating the cartoon strip for the *Daily Express* from 1935-1965 and continuing to draw the cover for the annual until 1973. Bestall had served in Flanders during World War I before studying at the Central School of Art and illustrating books for Enid Blyton, amongst others. Bestall brought a new dimension to the Rupert strips and annuals, utilising the scenery of North Wales and the Sussex Weald.

As president of the British Origami Society, Bestall regularly featured the art form in the Rupert annuals. He was appointed an MBE in 1985 and on his 93rd birthday received a message from Prince Charles:
'I have heard that you were sadly unable to receive your MBE from the Queen recently. I wanted to send you my congratulations on your award and to wish you a very happy birthday with many happy returns. As a child I well remember your marvellous illustrations of Rupert Bear.'

Bestall died the following year at Porthmadog, and in 2006 a blue plaque was erected at his home at Cranes Park Road, Surbiton, where he lived for thirty years.

Alfred Bestall was born in Mandalay, Burma, and another Burmese connection on the blue plaque front is Earl Mountbatten of Burma.

EARL MOUNTBATTEN
of BURMA

Born Prince Louis of Battenberg in 1900, at Frogmore House, Home Park, Windsor, Mountbatten was an uncle of Prince Philip, Duke of Edinburgh, and second cousin once removed of Elizabeth II. As a child, he visited and got to know the doomed Russian Imperial family and had romantic feelings towards his first cousin, Grand Duchess Maria, who was murdered with the rest of the Imperial family in 1918. He kept this photograph of her by his bedside for the rest of his life.

During the Second World War, he was Supreme Allied Commander, South East Asia Command, the last Viceroy of India and the first Governor-General of independent India from 1947. He supported fellow plaque recipient Noel Coward's 1942 film In Which We Serve, inspired by Mountbatten's exploits when he captained HMS Kelly. From 1954 he was First Sea Lord before becoming Chief of the Defence Staff until 1965, and also serving as Chairman of the NATO Military Committee.

In 1979, Mountbatten and his grandson Nicholas were killed by a bomb, placed in his fishing boat in Mullaghmore, County Sligo, by the Provisional IRA.

Mountbatten was appointed the Supreme Allied Commander, South East Asia Command, with promotion to Acting Full Admiral, by Winston Churchill.

WINSTON CHURCHILL

Born into the family of the Dukes of Marlborough, his father Randolph had been Chancellor of the Exchequer and his mother an American socialite. Churchill was educated at prep school in Lansdowne Road, Hove, Sussex before going on to Harrow.

Churchill saw action as a young army officer in British India, the Anglo-Sudan War, and the Second Boer War. Before World War I, he served as President of the Board of Trade, Home Secretary and First Lord of the Admiralty, continuing the latter until the disastrous Gallipoli campaign.

He later served under Lloyd George as Minister of Munitions, Secretary of State for War, Secretary of State for Air, and Secretary of State for the Colonies. In the second half of the 1920s, he was Chancellor of the Exchequer under Stanley Baldwin, but his opposition to Indian home rule, and his resistance to the abdication of Edward VIII, left him in the political wilderness for the rest of the 1930s.

Churchill was pro-rearmament and a strong voice in warning of the potential danger from Hitler's Nazi Germany. Following the resignation of Neville Chamberlain in 1940, Churchill became Prime Minister, with his patriotic speeches and radio broadcasts lifting the spirit of both the nation and those fighting for its freedom. He led Britain until the German surrender in 1945, but suffered a surprise defeat in the 1945 general election.

As leader of the opposition, he was again extremely vocal, this time over concern with Soviet influence in Europe. The 1951 general election saw him Prime Minister for a second period, which was dominated by foreign affairs such as Mau Mau terrorists, Malaya, the Korean War and the UK-backed coup d'état in Iran.

Churchill retired as Prime Minister in 1955, but remained an MP until 1964, having, a year earlier, been the first of only eight people to have been made an honorary citizen of the United States. He was no mean painter either, with 15 of his paintings selling for £11.2 million in 2014.

The phrase OMG is now widely used, especially in social media, but in September 1917 Churchill was the recipient of a letter from Lord Fisher, using OMG for the first time in print. Having turned down the Queen's offer of giving him the title Duke of London, Sir Winston Leonard Spencer-Churchill KG OM CH TD PC PCc DL FRS RA died, aged ninety, in 1965, was granted a state funeral, and in 2002 was named the Greatest Briton of all time.

Viscountess Astor was noted for exchanges with Winston Churchill. Churchill is supposed to have told Lady Astor that having a woman in Parliament was like having one intrude on him in the bathroom, to which she retorted, 'You're not handsome enough to have such fears'. Lady Astor is also said to have responded to a question from Churchill about what disguise he should wear to a masquerade ball by saying, 'Why don't you come sober, Prime Minister?' In another famously recounted exchange, Lady Astor said to Churchill, 'If you were my husband, I'd poison your tea', to which he responded, 'Madam, if you were my wife, I'd drink it'.

NANCY ASTOR

In 1919, Nancy Witcher Langhorne Astor, Viscountess Astor, CH, became the first female Member of Parliament to take a seat in the house. An American citizen, she moved to England at the age of 26, where she married newspaper proprietor Waldorf Astor, his father giving them Clivedon as a wedding present. She went into politics after her husband had succeeded to the peerage and entered the House of Lords. She served in Parliament until 1945.

Astor was hampered in the popular campaign for her known opposition to alcohol consumption and her ignorance of current political issues. Her tendency to say odd or outlandish things sometimes made her appear unstable. On one occasion, while canvassing in Plymouth, she was greeted at a door by a young girl whose mother was away. As Astor was unfamiliar with the area, she had been given a naval officer as an escort. The girl said about her mother, 'But she said if a lady comes with a sailor they're to use the upstairs room and leave ten bob' (50 pence today).

She is commemorated with a blue plaque unveiled in 1987 at 4 St. James's Square.

 Nancy Astor was great friends with George Bernard Shaw from the late 1920s until Shaw's death in 1950, the pair exchanging well over 250 letters.

GEORGE BERNARD SHAW

Born in Dublin in 1856, George Bernard Shaw moved to London at the age of twenty-one, becoming a major influence on theatre, culture and, to an extent, politics, as a prominent member of the Fabian Society. He penned more than sixty plays including *Arms and the Man*, *Man and Superman* and *Pygmalion*, the latter being adapted for the stage and film as *My Fair Lady*. It was first filmed, though, as *Pygmalion*, for which Shaw provided the screenplay in 1938, receiving an Academy Award.

Considered to be the leading dramatist of his generation, Shaw was awarded the Nobel Prize for Literature in 1925. His strong views against organised religion, his blaming Britain as well as Germany for WWI and his declared admiration for such dictators as Mussolini and Stalin, would have created outrage and disgust through today's media and social media, but back in the day it barely affected the popularity of his works.

Shaw refused all honours, including an Order of Merit, offered to him in 1946, just four years before his death.

George Bernard Shaw was awarded the Nobel prize for Literature in 1925 while the Nobel prize for Physiology or Medicine in 1945 went to Sir Alexander Fleming, who shared it with Ernst Boris Chain and Sir Howard Walter Florey.

ALEXANDER FLEMING

Fleming, a Scottish physician, biologist, phramacologist and botanist, is best-known for discovering the world's first antibiotic, Penicillin G., which turned out to be the most efficacious life-saving drug in the world. Its estimated that penicillin has saved somewhere in the region of 200,000,000 lives and continues to help millions around the world, helping to combat gangrene, tuberculosis and syphilis.

Highly knowlegable on bacteria, immunisatio, and chemotherapy, Fleming was knighted for has achievements in 1944. Oxford University scientists Howard Florey and Ernst Chain played an important role in helping to realise penicillin's full potential a decade after its discovery.

He wrote many articles on bacteriology, immunology, and chemotherapy and in 2009 was voted third 'Greatest Scot' behind Robert Burns and

William Wallace. Fleming also featured in *Time Magazine*'s 100 Most Important People of the 20th Century' and appeared in the BBC's poll '100 Greatest Britons.' A blue plaque adorns the front wall of St Mary's Hospital, Paddington.

In 2017 a swatch of mould, said to be the one from which Fleming created penicillin, sold for almost £12,000 at auction. On an architectural note, the man whose discovery would change the course of history has the Alexander Fleming Building in South Kensington and two public houses named after him.

The poet John Betjeman also has a road named after him in Marlborough and pub named after him on St Pancras station. Betjeman also has a statue at the terminus, as he was instrumental in saving the station from demolition.

JOHN BETJEMAN

Educated at Highgate School, The Dragon School, Marlborough and Magdalen College Oxford, in 1972 Sir John Betjeman succeeded Cecil Day-Lewis to become the UK's Poet Laureate until his death in 1984. His volumes of poetry include *Mount Zion, Continual Dew, Old Lights for New Chancels, New Bats in Old Belfries, A Few Late Chrysanthemums, Poems in the Porch, A Nip in the Air*, and the autobiographical epic *Summoned by Bells*. His non-fiction works include *Ghastly Good Taste, An Oxford University Chest, English Cities* and *Small Towns and the Shell Guides*.

A passionate member of the Victorian Society, he helped to save Bedford Park and St Pancras Station, he described himself in Who's Who as a 'poet and a hack.' He was created a CBE in 1960, awarded the Queen's Medal for Poetry made a Companion of Literature, the Royal Society of Literature, and was created a Knight Bachelor in 1969. In 2011, the University of Oxford honoured Betjeman by declaring him one of its 100 most distinguished members from ten centuries.

Betjeman made albums of his poems with Jim Parker, with the spoken word over the music, and David Essex took Betjeman's *Myfanwy* into the music charts in 1987.

Betjeman studied at Marlborough College in the 1920s, and singer/songwriter Nick Drake was a pupil there in the 1960s.

NICK DRAKE

Betjeman was at Marlborough College in the 1920s, dreaming of becoming a poet. Forty years later, in the 1960s, Nick Drake was at Marlborough hoping to become a successful singer/songwriter. He went there from Eagle House prep school in Berkshire. His French teacher, John Watson, wrote the song that came second in the 1960 Eurovision Song Contest, *Looking High, High, High*. Perhaps he inspired the young Drake, and perhaps his own inspiration for the song come from the school motto *Sublimiora Petamus* (Aiming High/Let Us Seek Higher Things).

Nick Drake signed to Island Records while studying at Cambridge University, but became increasingly introverted and seemed to find it ever more difficult to cope with the world, despite his family trying to understand his problems and help him as much as they could.

Albums such as *Five Leaves Left*, *Bryter Later* and *Pink Moon* continue to inspire and delight new generations of writers and musicians. Whether by accident or design, Nick Drake took his own life in 1974 at the age of twenty-six. No live footage of Nick Drake performing has ever emerged, but many artists have cited him as a major musical influence.

Drake's producer, Joe Boyd, also worked on Sandy Denny's records; both Nick and Sandy were awarded blue plaques for BBC Music Day in 2017.

SANDY DENNY

Alexandre Elene Maclean 'Sandy' Denny was the lead singer with the folk rock band Fairport Convention during 1968 and 1969, having previously performed with The Strawbs.

She left Fairport to form Fotheringay in 1970, then briefly rejoined Fairport before focusing on a solo career and releasing four albums between 1971 and 1977. She also duetted with Robert Plant on *The Battle of Evermore*, a track on the album Led Zeppelin IV. Possibly her most enduring song, *Who Knows Where the Time Goes*, has been recorded by many artists, including Judy Collins, Nina Simone, and 10,000 Maniacs.

Her blue plaque was unveiled by Bob Stanley from St. Etienne at Byfield Village Hall, where she played her final gig on April 1st 1978. Bob Stanley commented: 'It's a great honour for me to be unveiling this blue plaque on BBC Music Day, to the writer of the wonderful *Who Know Where the Time Goes*, and a singer with an uncommonly beautiful voice, the greatest of her generation... Sandy Denny.'

Sandy Denny was the singer with Fairport Convention before forming her own group, Fotheringay, named after Fotheringay Castle, the birthplace of Richard III.

RICHARD III

Richard was named Lord Protector for the son and successor to Edward IV, but after the Edward's death his marriage to Elizabeth Woodville was declared invalid, making their children illegitimate, and therefore ineligible for the throne. This left the way clear for Richard to be crowned. The would-be king and his brother were never seen again, giving rise to the legend of the Princes in the Tower, and their assumed murder by Richard.

Richard was King of England from 1483 until his defeat and demise, at the age of thirty-two, at the hands of Henry Tudor in 1485 at the Battle of Bosworth Field, during the Wars of the Roses. The last of the Plantagenet dynasty, he was also the last English King to die in battle on English soil.

Richard's body was buried at Leicester, the exact whereabouts unknown for more than five centuries until an excavation in 2012, on a site once occupied by the Greyfriars Monks, yielded a skeleton that would be identified as Richard III. His remains were reburied in Leicester Cathedral in March 2015.

 Richard III was of one of Shakespeare's histories, written in around 1592 and arguably the most famous actor to play the role of Shakespeare's Richard III was Sir Laurence Olivier.

LAURENCE OLIVIER

The son of a clergyman, Olivier was born in 1907 in Dorking and first came to prominence in Noel Coward's *Private Lives*, appearing in his first film, *Romeo and Juliet*, alongside John Gielgud and Peggy Ashcroft in 1935. Olivier became one of the giants of British theatre of the mid-20th century also also performing in more than fifty films as well as being a co-director of the Old Vic.

He was also the founding director of the National Theatre, where he continued to find acclaim as an actor, taking the title role in Othello and as appearing as Shylock in *The Merchant of Venice*.

He was made a knight in 1947, created a life peer in 1970, and received the Order of Merit. His acting achievements included four Academy Awards, two British Academy Film Awards, five Emmy Awards and three Golden Globes. He is commemorated in the prestigious Olivier Awards.

Baron Olivier was married three times, firstly to Jill Esmond from 1930-1940, Vivien Leigh from 1940-1960, and Joan Plowright from 1961 until his death in 1989. He allegedly came out with a wonderful line as the end drew near, saying 'This is one old ham that can't be cured.'

LAURENCE OLIVIER
ACTOR
1907-1989
WAS
BORN HERE

D & D P S

Olivier's second wife, Vivien Leigh, was also highly successful on the English stage and on the silver screen.

VIVIEN LEIGH

Born in Darjeeling, India in 1913 as Vivien Mary Hartley, Leigh's film career began in 1935, although she was considered primarily a stage performer. Leigh played roles created by two other blue plaque recipients, Noël Coward and George Bernard Shaw. Vivien Leigh became known as Lady Olivier after 1947.

She won two Academy Awards for Best Actress for her iconic performances as Scarlett O'Hara in the 1939 film *Gone with the Wind* and as Blanche DuBois in the film version of *A Streetcar Named Desire* in 1951, a role she'd already played on the London stage. She also won a Tony Award for her work in the 1963 Broadway musical *Tovarich*, and was an acclaimed beauty, but suffered from both recurring tuberculosis and bipolar disorder and died at the age of fifty-three.

In 1999, the American ilm Institute ranked her the 16th greatest female movie star of classic Hollywood cinema.

*Vivien Leigh's character in **Gone With the Wind**, Scarlett O'Hara, was adopted by songwriter Jerry Lordan as the title of the follow-up to his tune **Diamonds**, which was a No.1 for former Shadows Jet Harris and Tony Meehan.*

JERRY LORDAN

Scarlett O'Hara reached No. 2 in the charts in an era when Jerry Lordan had the golden touch. He also penned Jet and Tony's hit *Applejack* and *A Girl Like You* for Cliff Richard. His most enduring hits were *Apache* and *Wonderful Land*, both long-running No. 1s for The Shadows, the latter becoming a massive hit for Joran Ingmann in the US. Another big Shadows hit, *Atlantis*, was also a Jerry Lordan tune, as was one of their rare hits to feature vocals, *Mary Anne*.

A self-taught musician, he was born Jeremiah Lordan in Paddington, educated in Finchley, and served in the Royal air Force. His first success a a songwriter came in 1958 with *A House, a Car and a Wedding Ring*, and *I've Waited So Long*, a top three hit for Anthony Newley. Lordan was signed as an artist to Parlophone and had a few self-penned hits of his own, including *Who Could Be Bluer,* produced by George Martin, but was far more successful writing for Cliff Richard, The Shadows, Jet Harris and Tony Meehan, and other artists including Shane Fenton and Prince Philip's god-daughter, Louise Cordet.

Lordan penned a number of successful hits for The Shadows, a band whose members included Bruce Welch and Brian Bennett.

BRUCE WELCH
& BRIAN BENNETT

Two members of The Shadows were commemorated in 2017 for BBC Music Day, when a blue plaque was unveiled at the Globe, Stockton. This was where Bruce Welch and Brian Bennett wrote the iconic title song for the film *Summer Holiday*, which starred Cliff Richard, in the orchestra pit at the theatre. A children's ukulele massed band performed the song at the unveiling ceremony, at which Brian and Bruce unveiled the plaque. They recalled the moment they had written the song, fifty-five years earlier.

Brian: 'I was practising on an upright piano and Bruce was on the stage with his acoustic guitar, and this script arrived for this new movie *Summer Holiday* and Bruce said, they want a title song ; we wrote it there and then.'

Bruce: 'It's about these guys going through Europe on a London bus, who are going on a summer holiday... I had my acoustic guitar on and just came out with the first line, 'We're all going on a summer holiday...' And

Brian came out with the other part...'

Brian: ' "We're going were the sun shines brightly, we're going where the sea is blue." It was instant. You don't have to mess around with a song like that. It sort of came out of the sky.'

Bruce: 'Seriously. we had no idea that this song would last.'

Brian: 'When I saw the plaque and it said "Iconic song", I thought, I guess it is!'

Bruce: 'I've been telling you that for fifty years!'

Cliff Richard added his tribute to the song: 'How lucky can a singer get? Even now if I go to visit a school, which I've done many, many times, I'm thinking "they won't even know who I am," and then I get my guitar out and sing *Summer Holiday* and they all join in. 'Cause they've all been in the car with dad and mum going off on holiday. So to be connected with a song like that for me is just a dream. Absolutely fantastic.'

BBC Music Day

BRUCE WELCH & BRIAN BENNETT

wrote the iconic song
SUMMER HOLIDAY for
Cliff Richard & the Shadows
at this theatre in 1962

Awarded by
BBC Tees

British Plaque Trust

*As well as **Summer Holiday** and several other films, Cliff also starred in the stage version of **Heathcliff**, based on the original book by Emily Brontë, who is commemorated both with her own plaque and as a member of the Brontë family.*

THE BRONTËS

The solitary and reclusive Emily Brontë, to whom freedom was the essence of life, wrote under the pen name of Ellis Bell. She was born in 1818, in Thornton, near Bradford, and was the fifth of six children. The family moving to Haworth Priory where the Brontë girls were to develop their incredible literary talents. Her only novel, *Wuthering Heights*, was published in 1847, just a year before her death.

The youngest Brontë sister, Anne, writing under the name of Acton Bell, had her novel, *The Tenant of Wildfell Hall*, published in 1848, and Charlotte, under the pen name of Currer Bell had *Jane Eyre* published the previous year.

Charlotte has plaques in both Manchester and Filey. Anne, Emily and their brother Branwell all died within a few months of each other, leaving Charlotte as the longest surviving Brontë.

Jane Eyre, *Charlotte Bronte's novel dealing with the emancipation of women, was written in 1847, the year that champion of women's rights, leader of the match girls' strike, and social reformer Annie Besant was born.*

ANNIE BESANT

ANNIE BESANT AND THE MATCHWORKERS' COMMITTEE

Annie Besant was born at 39, Colby Road, Gipsy Hill in London.
One of Besant's two plaques is on the entrance gate to the Fairfield Match
Works, Bow. A socialist, writer, women's rights activist and orator, Besant
was also a fervent supporter of Irish Home Rule and Indian home rule.
Although she married and had two children, her strong anti-religious
views led to separation after just six years.

In 1877 Besant and her friend Charles Bardlaugh were prosecuted for
publishing a book on birth control, which brought them both a certain
notoriety. Besant went on to be a serious union activist, being one of
the leaders of the 10,000-strong 1887 Bloody Sunday march against
unemployment and coercion in Ireland. Many demonstrators, armed
with gas pipes, knives, pokers and iron bars clashed with the police who
arrested 400 marchers with seventy-five being badly hurt. Besant spoke at
the rally and offered herself for arrest, but the police refused to take her
into custody.

As well as being a leading speaker for the Fabian Society and the Marxist Social Democratic Federation, the following year she became embroiled in the famous match girls' strike, championing the women and girls working in poor conditions at the Bryant and May factory in Bow, East London.

Sparked by the dismissal of one of the girls, the workers were sick of fourteen-hour days, little pay and the severe health problems brought about by working in close proximity with white phosphorous. On the first day of the strike, some 1,400 women refused to work, resulting in the company offering to re-instate the sacked worker. But Annie Besant and the workforce had the bit between their teeth, and demanded Bryant and May ease up on the regular fines imposed on the girls. By 9th July the whole factory was on strike and the place came to a standstill, which is when a deputation went to Annie Besant for assistance.

She spoke on their behalf, brought their plight to the attention of parliament, created publicity, involved the London Trades Council, and helped to broker an agreement between the company and the workers. Her actions led to better working conditions, better pay, better eating facilities and eventually the abolition of white phosphorous.

 Annie Besant was a passionate advocate of Irish home rule, a notion she shared with British Prime Minister William Ewart Gladstone.

WILLIAM EWART GLADSTONE

Like Annie Besant, William Ewart Gladstone was a champion of Irish home rule, proposing it early in 1886, but found himself defeated in the House of Commons. The resulting split in the Liberal Party helped keep them out of office for the best part of the next twenty years. Born in 1809, Gladstone first entered Parliament in 1832, serving in Sir Robert Peel's Tory cabinet, until the split in the party resulted in him becoming a Peelite. The Peelites merged with the Radicals and Whigs to form the Liberal Party with

Gladstone as Chancellor of the Exchequer. During the 1850s Gladstone lived at Carlton Terrace, where there is a blue plaque commemorating his time at No.11 where he lived from 1857-1875. He'd previously resided at No.4 in 1856.

He served as Chancellor four times and as Prime Minister on four separate occasions, 1869-74, 1880-85, February-July 1886 and 1892-94 resigning at the age of eighty-four. During his first ministry he oversaw many reforms including the disestablishment of the Church of Ireland and the introduction of a secret ballot for elections. His second term was decidedly brief. After his proposal for Irish Home Rule was defeated in the Commons, a split was created in the Liberal Party which basically kept them out of power, with one short break, for almost twenty years. During Gladstone's last government, the second Irish Home Rule Bill passed the Commons but was defeated in the Lords.

Gladstone resigned in March 1894, in opposition to increased naval expenditure. He left parliament in 1895 and died three years later aged 88. Affectionately known by his supporters as 'The People's William' or the 'Grand Old Man,' or, according to Disraeli, 'God's Only Mistake,' Gladstone is considered to be one of our greatest Prime Ministers, despite being disliked by Queen Victoria, who much preferred Disraeli, the latter being one of the very few to be allowed to sit in her presence. Even in his eighties, Gladstone had to stand. Gladstone shares a blue plaque at 10 St James's Square with William Pitt and the Earl of Derby, all three of them living at the address at different times.

It had been back in 1840 when Gladstone first began his mission to rescue and rehabilitate London prostitutes, his actions being held to question in some areas. Later that decade he began conversing and consorting more closely with the 'fallen' women near the Argyll Rooms, their names regularly appearing in his diary. Many of the ladies were invited to the Gladstone's home, his mission being to save them by finding a suitable husband, through emigration or through gainful employment. For whatever reason, he admitted that he deliberately 'courted evil.' In being so close to temptation he also confessed that he 'trod the path of danger,'

 Fellow Victorian and blue plaque recipient Charles Dickens also, like Gladstone, had a penchant for helping 'fallen women.'

CHARLES DICKENS

In the late 1840s Angela Burdett-Coutts, heiress to the Coutts banking fortune, appeared keen to do something philanthropic for society. She decided on a home for fallen women and enlisted the help of her friend, Charles Dickens. The writer found what he felt was a suitable property in Lime Grove, Shepherd's Bush, then on the western fringes of London. Able to accommodate thirteen inmates and two superintendents, it opened in 1847 with Burdett-Coutts and Dickens insisting that the running of it should not be as harsh and draconian as similar institutions. Dickens was mainly responsible for the selection of suitable candidates, interviewing them, choosing the staff, looking after the accounts and even writing a pamphlet, *An Appeal to Fallen Women*:

'In this home, which stands in a pleasant country lane and where each may have her little flower-garden if she pleases, they will be treated with the greatest kindness; will lead an active, cheerful and healthy life; will learn many things it is profitable and good to know and being entirely removed from all who have any knowledge of their past career will begin life afresh and be able to win a good name and character.'

Between 1847 and 1858, when Dickens' involvement ended, it's believed that some hundred women 'graduated' from Lime Grove, many of them heading off for a new life in the colonies. In 1914, the purpose-built Gaumont Lime Grove film studio complex was built next door to Urania Cottage, the erstwhile home set up by Charles Dickens later being incorporated into the expansion of the studio which was used by the BBC from 1949-1991 and demolished in 1993. It is now part of a modern housing estate.

Aside from his philanthropy, Dickens remains one of the most successful and best-known authors in the English language through his classics: *The Pickwick Papers*, *Oliver Twist*, *Nicholas Nickleby*, *The Old Curiosity Shop*, *Barnaby Rudge*, *Martin Chuzzlewit*, *Dombey and Son*, *David Copperfield*, *Bleak House*, *Hard Times*, *Little Dorrit*, *A Tale of Two Cities*, *Great Expectations*, *Our Mutual Friend* and *The Mystery of Edwin Drood*. *Bleak House* was his bestseller during his lifetime, followed by *Dombey and Son*, *Little Dorrit* and *David Copperfield*. *A Tale of Two Cities* alone has now sold over 200,000,000 copies. On Dickens' death in 1870, The Times commented 'The loss of such a man is an event which makes ordinary expressions of regret seem cold and conventional.'

There are 47 plaques commemorating Charles Dickens.

*At the very beginning of the 1860s, **Great Expectations** sold an incredible 100,000 copies a week in the magazine **All The Year Round**. The first film of the book, directed by David Lean over eighty years later, starred John Mills as Pip, alongside Jean Simmons, Bernard Miles and Alec Guinness.*

JOHN MILLS

Sir John Mills CBE made his debut in 1929 at the London Hippodrome, and his film debut three years later in *The Midshipmaid*. In a career spanning seven decades, he appeared in over 120 films and won the Academy Award for Best Supporting Role in *Ryan's Daughter*.

In 1939 he starred in *Goodbye Mr. Chips* and his 1940s films included *In Which We Serve*, *Great Expectations*, *Waterloo Road*, *Way to the Stars*, and *Scott of the Antarctic*. In the 1950s he starred in *The Colditz Story*, *Above Us the Waves*, *Dunkirk*, *I Was Monty's Double* and *Ice Cold in Alex*. The latter film called for him to down a pint of a lager in one go; after six takes, filming had to be abandoned for the day! His 1970s films included *The Parent Trap* (in which he co-starred with his daughter Hayley), *Oh What a Lovely War*, *Ryan's Daughter*, and *The Family Way*.

In 2001, Mills and his wife, Mary Hayley Bell, reaffirmed their marriage vows after at their village church in Denham. He explained: 'I'm madly in love with her, you see.' Sir John Mills died in 2005, aged 97.

A blue plaque to John Mills was unveiled by his daughters, Juliet and Hayley with Robin Gibb and Mike Read, the then President and Vice-President of the Heritage Foundation. As president for some years, Robin was not only a leading light in the successful fight for an RAF Memorial, he also helped to unveil many plaques, including one for his own group, the Bee Gees, in 2008.

ROBIN GIBB
& THE BEE GEES

Robin Hugh Gibb and his twin Maurice were born on the Isle of Man in 1949, the family moving to Manchester and then emigrating to Brisbane. It was there that Robin and Maurice, together with older brother Barry, began singing, performing live and writing their own songs.

Having started recording as the Bee Gees, they returned to the UK where they started what was to become an incredible writing and recording career, with *New York Mining Disaster 1941*.

Hits such as *Massachusetts*, *Words*, *First of May* and *I've Gotta Get A Message To You* established them as both artists and songwriters in what was to be the first phase of their career. Robin went solo for a short while, notching up a No. 2 hit with *Saved By The Bell*.

With the songs not getting as high in the charts as many of their earlier hits, they moved from the sentimental to the disco with such songs as *Jive Talkin'*, *Stayin' Alive*, *How Deep Is Your Love*, *Night Fever*, *Tragedy*, *You Should Be Dancin'*, *Spirits Having Flown*, *Grease* and *Nights*

On Broadway. It was landing the soundtrack for the film that was to become *Saturday Night Fever* that re-established them and sent their sales soaring.

In the 1980s, they provided classic songs for other artists such as *Heartbreaker* and *Islands in the Stream* as well as re-establishing themselves yet again, with the 1987 No. 1 *You Win Again*. Robin's final project, with his son, R-J, was the *Titanic Requiem* which was performed a month before his death by the Royal Philharmonic Orchestra and included the haunting *Don't Cry Alone*.

Robin last performed on stage in February 2012 at the London Palladium with The Soldiers, passing away just three months later.

 *Robin was so grateful to broadcaster Alan Freeman for supporting his releases during his solo period that after Alan's death, Robin wrote and recorded a beautiful song about him called **Alan Freeman Days**. There is a plaque to Alan on Brinsworth House, the showbusiness care home in Twickenham.*

ALAN FREEMAN

Alan Freeman, known affectionately as 'Fluff' was born in New South Wales, Australia in 1927 where he had ideas about becoming an opera singer, but as his voice wasn't strong enough, he began working as a radio announcer on the teenager's station, 7LA in Tasmania. He then broadcast for 3KZ in Melbourne before travelling the world and settling in London.

His first programmes in the northern hemisphere were for Radio Luxembourg, for whom he would continue to present until the early 1970s. In 1960 he was taken on by the BBC Light Programme to present *Records Around Five*, using what would become his signature tune, *At the Sign of the Swinging Cymbal*. Freeman began presenting *Pick of the Pops* in 1961 as part of the radio show *Trad Tavern* until it became a programme in its own right in 1962. He would present it until 1972 as well as being a part of the original *Top of the Pops* presentation team, presenting other TV shows, and being a regular panellist on *Juke Box Jury*.

In 1972 he became a daily presenter on Radio One as well as hosting *Quiz Kid* and a rock show for five years, leaving at the end of the decade to join Capital Radio. In 1989 he returned to the BBC, reviving *Pick of the Pops* and *The Rock Show*, went again in the Radio One cull, only to return in 1997 after spells at stations such as Capital and Virgin.

He was awarded the MBE in 1998 and also appeared in several films, including *Absolute Beginners*, *It's Trad Dad*, *Just for Fun*, and *Sebastian*.

He was the subject of *This Is Your Life* in 1987 and was also well-known for fronting TV commercials for OMO washing powder and Brentford Nylons. With his much-loved catchphrases, 'All right, stay bright,' 'Not 'arf,' 'Greeting music lovers' and 'Hi there, Pop Pickers', he hosted *Pick of the Pops* until 2000 when his arthritis got the better of him. 'Fluff' died in 2006 and is commemorated with a blue plaque at Brinsworth House, the nursing and residential home for theatre and entertainment professionals.

 In 1965, Alan Freeman played Bill Rogers in **Dr. Terror's House of Horrors**, *alongside Christopher Lee and Peter Cushing.*

PETER CUSHING

Peter Wilton Cushing was born in Kenley, Surrey in 1913 and briefly followed his father to become a surveyor, before enrolling at the Guildhall School of Music and Drama. He performed in repertory before heading to Hollywood in 1939 and making his first film, *The Man in the Iron Mask*. He made several other films, including *A Chump at Oxford* with Laurel and Hardy, before returning home to contribute to the war effort by joining ENSA.

After the war he appeared in the West End with Laurence Olivier in Hamlet, but a decade later he'd become synonymous with the horror films produced by Hammer. His first roles for the company were *The Curse of Frankenstein*, *The Horror of Dracula* and Sherlock Holmes in *The Hound of the Baskervilles*. In the mid-1960s he played the Doctor in the films *Dr. Who and the Daleks* and *Daleks - Invasion Earth*. Despite being best-known for horror movies, Cushing also appeared in *Star Wars Episode IV: A New Hope* and his final film before retirement, *Biggles: Adventures in Time*.

Cushing, a BAFTA Award winner, died in 1994 in Canterbury and has a blue plaque on his home in Whitstable, and a plaque on a pub which was named after him.

 Peter Cushing not only played Sherlock Holmes several times on film and on BBC television, but he was also a devoted fan of the character. The genius detective was, of course, the creation of Sir Arthur Conan Doyle.

SIR ARTHUR CONAN DOYLE

Born in 1859, Sir Arthur Ignatius Conan Doyle KStJ. DL. was a physician who turned to writing, first creating Sherlock Holmes and his loyal sidekick Dr. Watson. The first of four novels, *A Study in Scarlet,* was published in 1887, and Conan Doyle would write over fifty short stories about the crime fighter who resided in London at 221B Baker Street.

A story that must have intrigued the thirteen-year-old Conan Doyle was that of the ghost ship the Mary Celeste, found abandoned between the Azores and Portugal in 1872, as he introduced a link in one of his stories. In The Sussex Vampire, when Holmes receives a letter mentioning Matilda Briggs, he explains to Watson: 'Matilda Briggs was not the name of a young woman... It was a ship which is associated with the giant rat of Sumatra, a story for which the world is not yet prepared.' In reality, Sophia Matilda Briggs was the two-year-old daughter of the captain of the Mary Celeste who, along with the rest of those on board, disappeared without trace.

Conan Doyle played in goal for Portsmouth AFC as A.C. Smith, the team being a precursor of Portsmouth FC, who also have a blue plaque, commemorating their foundation in 1898. Also a first class cricketer, the only wicket Conan Doyle took at that level was that of the great batsman W.G. Grace, while playing for the MCC at Crystal Palace in 1900. The batting doctor mistimed a shot from the bowling doctor and was caught by the wicket-keeper. Conan Doyle was so thrilled that he wrote a poem about it, featuring the lines:

I captured that glorious wicket
The greatest, the grandest of all.

Conan Doyle is said to have created the name Sherlock from fellow MCC player, Frank Shacklock and his fellow Nottinghamshire team-mate Mordecai Sherwin, while it is presumed that the character of Holmes is based on Joseph Bell, Doyle's university teacher. Conan Doyle wrote in a letter to him: 'It is most certainly to you that I owe Sherlock Holmes...' Conan Doyle wrote the first five Holmes short stories from his office at 2 Upper Wimpole Street (then known as Devonshire Place), which is now marked by a memorial plaque.

Not only a doctor, author, footballer and cricketer, Conan Doyle was a pioneer of cross-country skiing, correctly predicting in the *Strand* magazine in 1894 that he was 'convinced that there will come a time when hundreds of Englishmen will come to Switzerland for the 'skiing' season.'

Following his death in 1930 the Spiritualist Association rented the Albert Hall for a mass séance, with a 10,000 strong audience hoping that clairvoyant Estelle Roberts could reach the newly-departed spirit of Sherlock Holmes' creator.

*One of Sir Arthur Conan Doyle's plaques is shared with Oscar Wilde. The authors dined together with their mutual publisher at the Langham Hotel in August 1889, a meeting that led to Conan Doyle writing **The Sign of Four** and Wilde **The Picture of Dorian Gray**.*

OSCAR WILDE

Five years Conan Doyle's senior, Oscar Fingal O'Flahertie Wills Wilde was born in Dublin in 1854 and went on to study at Trinity and Magdalen College, Oxford, where he read the Greats.

Known as a great raconteur, aesthete and wit, his epigrams became enormously popular, as would his plays. He undertook a lengthy speaking tour of the United States and Canada, published a book of poems and dressed in a dandified and affected style.

By the early 1890s, he had become one of London's best-known personalities and most popular playwrights. His 1891 play *Salome* was refused a licence in England as biblical subjects were prohibited, but he took the theatrical world by storm with his four society comedies, *Lady Windermere's Fan*, *An Ideal Husband*, *A Woman of no Importance*, and *The Importance of Being Earnest*.

In 1895 Wilde was at the height of his fame, but disaster lurked in the shape of his selfish and manipulative young lover, Lord Alfred Douglas AKA Bosie. Douglas's father, Lord Queensberry, incensed at his son's affair with Wilde, left the latter an inflammatory note at Wilde's club, but instead of taking sound advice from more genuine friends such as Robbie Ross, Oscar let himself be goaded into legal action by Bosie.

He attempted, unsuccessfully, to sue Queensberry, but courtroom revelations began to point a finger at Wilde himself. His refusal to take the ensuing trial seriously and his flippancy in court possibly contributed to a determination to put him in gaol. He went down for 'gross indecency with men' and was sentenced to two years hard labour.

While in Reading Gaol he wrote *De Profundis*, a lengthy letter seemingly aimed at Bosie, published five years after his death, about his feelings and emotions. On release he left for France, writing *The Ballad of Reading Gaol* there in 1898.

Oscar Wilde died at L'Hotel in Rue Des Beax Arts in 1900 at the age of 46.

Oscar Wilde is not the only public figure to be celebrated by a blue plaque in Tite Street - so too, is Leslie Haden-Guest.

LESLIE HADEN-GUEST

Leslie Haden-Guest,1877-1960, was a physician, author and Labour politician. Born in Oldham, his father was a surgeon, physician and avid Labour supporter. After studying in Manchester and the London Hospital, he served in the Royal Army Medical Corps in the Boer War, WWI and even WWII, winning the Military Cross. The founder of the Anglo-French Committee of the Red Cross and the Labour Commonwealth Group, he became MP for Southwark North (1923-27) and Islington North (1937-50).

Created Baron Haden-Guest of Saling in 1950, he was also Lord-in-Waiting to King George VI and Assistant Opposition Whip in the House of Lords. He was the grandfather of actor, musician and director, Christopher Haden-Guest, now 5th Baron Haden-Guest, who has made many great films including *Spinal Tap*, *Break Like the Wind* and *Best in Show*.

Haden-Guest's terms as an MP were served under Clement Attlee who would become Prime Minister from 1945 until 1951.

CLEMENT ATTLEE

Born in 1883, Clement Attlee was first elected to Parliament in 1922, rising to become a junior minister and then a member of Ramsay MacDonald's Cabinet from 1929. The Labour Party were heavily defeated in the 1931 General Election, but Attlee kept his seat and became Deputy leader.

After the resignation of George Lansbury in 1935, Attlee was elected leader of the Labour Party and although he was an advocate for pacifism and opposed rearmament, he later changed his position, criticising Chamberlain's attempts to appease Hitler and Mussolini. In 1942 he was appointed Deputy Prime Minister during Churchill's Coalition Government, the two working extremely well together until the end of WWII in May 1945.

THE NEW

NATIONAL HEALTH SERVICE

Your new National Health Service begins on 5th July. What is it? How do you get it? It will provide you with all medical, dental, and nursing care. Everyone—rich or poor, man, woman or child—can use it or any part of it. There are no charges, except for a few special items. There are no insurance qualifications. But it is not a "charity". You are all paying for it, mainly as taxpayers, and it will relieve your money worries in time of illness.

Attlee led the Labour Party to win the 1945 Election with an unexpected, but huge, majority. He served as Prime Minister from 1945 to 1951 and as the leader of the Labour Party from 1935-1955.

Elevated to the Peerage in 1955, Clement Richard Attlee, 1st Earl Attlee, KG, OM, CH, PC, FRS, remains the longest-ever serving leader of the Labour Party. Under him, the National Health Service was created and much of Britain's infrastructure was nationalised, including the coal and steel industries. India was also granted its independance under the Attlee government.

Labour lost the General Election in 1951, and Attlee's career and the fortunes of his party declined. Ultimately unable to quell the infighting and division within the parliamentary Labour Party, Attlee resigned as leader in 1955.

Clement Attlee died on 8th October 1967. A blue plaque to commemorate him is situated on his former home at 17 Monkhams Avenue in Woodford Green in Redbridge.

Clement Attlee was an avid football fan and player. As a young man, he had played football for the non-league side Fleet FC in Hampshire; his aunt lived in a house that backed on to the ground. Attlee attended Wembley with HM The Queen and Prince Philip, watching Manchester United beat Leicester City 3-1 in the 1963 FA Cup Final. Bobby Charlton played in that match along with other survivors of the Munich Air Disaster. In 2016, Bobby Charlton unveiled a blue plaque at the Dudley birthplace of his former team-mate Duncan Edwards, who died following the Munich Air Disaster.

DUNCAN EDWARDS

Duncan Edwards was born in Woodside, Dudley, Warwickshire, in 1936, representing his school, local and district teams before being selected for trials in both the National Morris and Sword Dancing Festival and the English Schools Football Association Under-14 team. Both fell on the same day. Luckily for Manchester United and England, Edwards chose the latter trial. He made his debut for the England Schools XI v Wales in 1950, was then made captain and Joe Mercer, then coaching the England Schools team urged Matt Busby to sign the lad.

He signed for Manchester United as a teenager and became, at 16 years and 185 days, the youngest player to appear in the Football League's First Division, but started an apprenticeship as a carpenter to get a trade behind him in case his career as a professional footballer didn't take off. In 1953 Matt Busby brought in other young players such as Dennis Violett, Jackie Blanchflower and later Bobby Charlton to create a team that would become known as 'The Busby Babes'.

In a career lasting just five years, he helped United win two League titles and reach the semi-finals of the European Cup. In 1955 he made his full England debut at 18 years and 183 days, becoming the youngest England player since WWII, the record standing until Michael Owen's England debut in 1998. Edwards began his National Service in 1955 and was stationed with team-mate Bobby Charlton, but they were allowed leave to play in matches. Edwards was tipped to take over the England captaincy from Billy Wright, but it was not to be.

Edwards played his final game for Manchester United against Red Star Belgrade, his team progressing to the semi-finals of the European Cup. The plane bringing them home from Belgrade crashed on take-off after refuelling in Munich, with seven players and 14 other passengers dying at the scene. Edwards was taken to Rechts der Isar Hospital with multiple leg fractures, damaged kidneys and fractured ribs, but the doctors were confident that he'd recover. An artificial kidney proved problematical, but Edwards was still able to ask assistant manager Jimmy Murphy, 'What time is the kick-off against Wolves, Jimmy? I mustn't miss that match.'

His condition improved dramatically but then took a turn for the worse and he died on 21st February. More than 5,000 people lined the streets of Dudley for his funeral, and a street was later named in his honour.

Edwards was also portrayed on a set of 'Football Legends' stamps in 1996, and a blue plaque was unveiled by Bobby Charlton at the site of Edwards' former digs in Stretford. Charlton described him as 'The only player that made me feel inferior.'

The accolades from other players have been eulogistic, and Edwards was inducted into the English Football Hall of Fame in 2002.

Duncan Edwards is also commemorated with a statue and in two stained glass windows at St Francis's Church, the parish church for the Priory Estate where Edwards grew up.

Another blue plaque recipient commemorated in a stained glass window is Lt. Gen. Robert Stephenson Smyth Baden-Powell.

ROBERT BADEN-POWELL

Born in 1857, Baden-Powell was educated at Charterhouse and served in the British Army from 1876 in South Africa and India. It was in South Africa, during the Second Boer War, that he successfully defended the town in the Siege of Mafeking. His military books, written for scout reconnaissance and training in Africa, were eagerly read by boys too young to be in service, but who were inspired by its ideals and principles.

In 1907, he ran a practical demonstration scout camp on Brownsea Island, which sowed the seeds for the formation of the scouting movement. In 1908, Baden-Powell wrote highly popular *Scouting for Boys* and on retiring from the army he formed The Boy Scout Association, becoming their first Chief Scout. The first Scout Rally was held at Crystal Palace, with many girls turning up declaring that they were 'Girl Scouts' which led to the formation of the Girl Guides by Baden-Powell and his sister Agnes. He worked with the scouts until retiring in 1937 and he lived out his final years in Kenya.

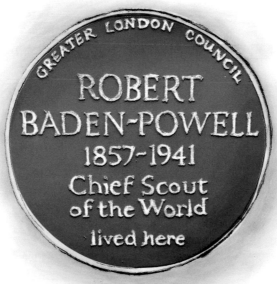

Baden-Powell was listed in Hitler's Sonderfahndungsliste G.B. (Special Search List Great Britain), the 'Black Book' compiled by Walter Schellenberg that listed the prominent people Hitler wanted to have arrested and interred after the proposed German invasion. Also in that list was Paul Robeson.

PAUL ROBESON

Paul Leroy Robeson was born in 1898, attended Rutgers College and became an outstanding American footballer, playing in the National football league and being inducted into the College Football Hall of Fame some eighty years later.

After college he embarked on a singing and acting career, recording songs from 1925 onwards across a whole range of genres. Robeson became a political activist, taking a stand against fascism, social injustice and through his affiliation with communism, and the advocacy of their policies, he was placed on the Attorney General's List of Subversive Organisations, investigated and subsequently blacklisted in the 1950s as part of the McCarthy witch hunt.

His passport was confiscated and his income dropped drastically; by the time his passport was returned his health was failing and he retired from public life.

*Robeson was unavailable to play the part of Joe in the original 1927 Broadway musical production of **Show Boat**, but he later starred in later US productions including the 1932 and 1940 revivals, and the 1936 film version, singing **Old Man River** and the duet **Ah Still Suits Me**. He also starred in the 1928 UK premiere of the show, his first appearance outside the United States. **Show Boat** was written by Oscar Hammerstein II and Jerome Kern.*

JEROME KERN

Jerome David Kern was born in New York in 1885 and went on to co-write dozens of Broadway musicals and compose more than 700 songs, including *Smoke Gets In Your Eyes*, *Ol' Man River*, *I've Told Every Little Star* and *The Way You Look Tonight*. He collaborated with many great lyricists and librettists, including Oscar Hammerstein II, Otto Harbach, Dorothy Fields, Johnny Mercer, PG Wodehouse and Ira Gershwin.

In 1909, while on a trip to England, Kern and some friends came up the River Thames and at Walton-on-Thames found themselves at the Swan Inn. Kern fell in love with Eva Leale, the landlord's daughter and stayed with them when he came to England. The following year Jerome Kern and Eva Leale were married in St Mary's Church, Walton-on-Thames.

Kern's plaque can be seen on the wall of The Swan Inn.

 Kern's plaque at the Swan Hotel Walton is a few yards away from the Manor House Walton, the home of John Bradshaw, who presided over the trial of Charles I, and where it's said that Oliver Cromwell signed Charles' death warrant.

OLIVER CROMWELL

Oliver Cromwell was born in Huntingdon in 1599, becoming their member of Parliament twenty-nine years later and later still, MP for Cambridge. Descended from the family of Henry VIII's minister, Thomas Cromwell, he underwent a religious conversion in the 1630s and became an Independent Puritan. Nicknamed 'Old Ironsides,' he fought with the Parliamentarians in the English Civil War and was swiftly promoted to a commanding role in the New Model Army. He was a signatory of Charles I's death warrant, defeated the Confederate and Royalist coalition in Ireland, occupied the country and then led a campaign against the Scots.

The Commonwealth displaced the monarchy from 1649 and by the end of 1653 Cromwell was invited to become Lord Protector of England, Scotland, and Ireland.

Cromwell died in 1658 and was buried at Westminster Abbey, his son Richard Cromwell inherited the position of Lord Protector, but resigned in 1659 with the army taking control and leaving him as Protector in name only. Richard Cromwell is the second longest-lived ruler of the country, dying at the age of eighty-five. With the Reformation, his father's body was exhumed, hung in chains and beheaded.

Oliver Cromwell was MP for Cambridge in 1640. His predecessor but one, Talbot Pepys held the same office from 1625. Pepys (1583-1666) was the great-uncle of diarist Samuel Pepys.

SAMUEL PEPYS

Samuel Pepys was born in 1633. He became an MP and rose to be Chief Secretary to the Admiralty, administrator of England's Navy, despite having no maritime experience. Rather unusually, Pepys kept a tame lion in his office at the Admiralty, sent to him by Algiers consul, Samuel Martin. He held the post under Charles II and James II, but remains best-known for his diary, which he kept from 1660 until 1669.

First published in the 19th century, it's an incredible eye-witness account of life in the decade, which documents the period of the Restoration, the Plague, the Great Fire of London and the Second Dutch War, as well as parochial day to day minutae and his witnessing of the execution of Charles I back in 1649. In the 1670s Pepys was arrested on trumped up charges of trying to restore James II to the throne, treason (accused of passing naval secrets to the French) and piracy (accused of plotting to plunder Dutch and English ships). Despite being sent briefly to the Tower, the charges came to nothing.

On a more pioneering note, Pepys designed his own spectacles, consisting of an elaborate face mask and tubes.

 Samuel Pepys died in 1703, but the most acclaimed diarist in British history made an appearance in the pop charts over two and a half centuries later, in 1961, with **Pepys' Diary***. The song was written and performed by Benny Hill.*

BENNY HILL

Benny Hill, one of Britain's best-loved comedians, was born Alfred Hawthorne Hill in 1924. He began working on radio after WWII. He first appeared on TV in 1950, in his first film, *Who Done It?* in 1956, and had his own regular cartoon strip in the children's comic, *Radio Fun*. He had his own TV sitcom from 1962-63, and had a radio series on the BBC Light programme from 1964-66. Hill also released many comedy pop singles, which often put him in the charts alongside major singers. *Gather in the Mushrooms*, *Pepys' Diary*, *Transistor Radio*, and *Harvest of Love* were all successful and boosted his popularity further, with his biggest musical success coming a few years later in 1971 when *Ernie (The Fastest Milkman in the West)* got to No.1.

As well as his radio, TV, and music careers, he also starred in the films *Light Up the Sky*, *Those Magnificent Men in Their Flying Machines*, *Chitty Chitty Bang Bang*, and *The Italian Job*. He is best remembered, though, for his phenomenally successful TV show, which not only pulled in colossally audiences (peaking at 21 million in 1971) but also transferred to the States, where he became almost as popular as he was in Britain.

 There are few comedians represented at the world-famous waxworks Madame Tussauds, but Benny Hill is one - and Charlie Chaplin is another.

CHARLIE CHAPLIN

The undisputed comedy king of the silent screen, Charles Spencer Chaplin was born in London in 1889 becoming a globally iconic figure, through his screen persona as 'The Tramp'.

Before a career lasting more than 75 years he was raised in poverty, spending two periods in the workhouse before he reached double figures. His mother being committed to a mental asylum was another blow, but he began performing at an early age, working in the music halls before signing with Fred Karno's company in 1908. After working with Karno in the States, Chaplin was offered film work with Keystone Studios, even being allowed to direct his own movies.

By the end of WWI he was one of the best-known figures in the world, and in 1919 co-founded United Artists. His first feature-length film was *The Kid* in 1921, with *A Woman of Paris*, *The Gold Rush* and *The Circus* all being released during the 1920s. Steadfastly refusing to adapt to sound he continued to produce silent films in the 'talkie' era and satirised Adolf Hitler in *The Great Dictator*.

His star waned after he was publicly involved in a paternity suit, went through marriages with much younger women, and was accused of having communist sympathies by the McCarthy regime. After an FBI investigation, one of America's most-loved comedians was forced to leave the country and live in Switzerland.

Nevertheless, he continued to make films, including *Limelight*, *A King in New York* and *A Countess from Hong Kong*. In 1972, as part of a renewed appreciation for his work, Chaplin received an Honorary Academy Award for 'the incalculable effect he has had in making motion pictures the art form of this century.'

Not only did Chaplin write, direct, produce and star in his own films, he also wrote the music. An excellent songwriter, he wrote such classics as *Limelight*, *This Is My Song* and *Smile*. Created a knight of the realm, Sir Charlie Chaplin KBE died on Christmas Day 1977.

Although he'd written the melody in the 1930s. Charlie Chaplin worked on the lyrics to **Smile** *at Peter Maurice Music in Denmark Street in 1954 ,with Jimmy Phillips (who wrote as John Turner) and Geoffrey Parsons.*

Next door, at No. 21 Denmark Street, was Lawrence Wright Music. He'd been the first publisher in the street in 1908, and wrote songs under the pen name of Horatio Nicholls.

LAWRENCE WRIGHT

Lawrence Wright, born on 15th February 1888, was a composer and publisher of popular music. Under the banner of The Wright Music Co., his first hit was *Don't Go Down The Mine, Daddy'* by William Geddes and Robert Donnelly (1910). In 1908, Wright set up a business office in Denmark Street, London.

Wright wrote many songs of his own, including *Down by the Stream*. Largely writing under his pen name of Horatio Nicholls, he wrote and co-wrote over 600 songs during his lifetime. His most famous composition is *Among My Souvenirs*, a familiar tune recorded my several big names including Frank Sinatra and Bing Crosby.

Wright founded *Melody Maker* magazine in 1926. He produced the annual production *On With the Show* at Blackpool for a staggering 32 Years. Wright was presented with an Ivor Novello Award in 1962 for outstanding service to British popular and light music'.

*Wright, under his pen name Horatio Nicholls, co-wrote **Amy** with J. G. Gilbert, a tribute song to pioneering aviator Amy Johnson, celebrating her flight between England to Australia in 1930.*

'Amy, wonderful Amy, I'm proud of the way you flew,
Believe me Amy you cannot blame me for falling in love with you.'

AMY JOHNSON

Born in Great Bridge Street, Tipton, Hull in 1903 in a house lit and heated by candles and oil lamps, Amy Johnson graduated from Sheffield University with a degree in Economics.

Whilst working as a legal secretary in London, she took up flying as a hobby, getting her pilot's licence in 1929, the same year she became the first woman to obtain a ground engineer's licence. In her de Havilland Gypsy Moth, *Jason*, she became the first woman to fly solo the 11,000 miles from England to Australia and receiving a cheque for £10,000 from the *Daily Mail* for her achievement.

She was awarded a CBE for her feat and the following year, with her co-pilot Jack Humphreys, in *Jason II*, became the first to fly to Moscow and back in one day. Any and Jack also set the record time for flying from the UK to Japan and she and went on to set many other long-distance records during the 1930s, including a solo record from London to Cape Town.

With her husband Jim Mollinson, a fellow pilot she married in 1932, she flew non-stop from the Pendine Sands in South Wales to the USA; the plane ran out of fuel and crash-landed in Connecticut. The couple then embarked on a record-breaking flight from Britain to India with Amy making her last record-breaking flight in regaining her London to Cape Town record, in 1936. Two years later, her tempestuous marriage ended in divorce.

At the outbreak of WWII Amy Johnson joined the Air Transport Auxiliary, rising to the rank of first officer, but on a flight from Blackpool to RAF Kidlington in 1941, her plane seemed to go off course in bad weather.

One source claimed that she bailed out but was drowned in the Thames Estuary and as late as 2011, historian Dr. Alec Gill suggested that her death was covered up after she'd been sucked into the propeller of the ship attempting to rescue her. This was based on the information from a witness on board the ship *HMS Haslemere*, who remembered the ship's engines being reversed, which may have caused her to be pulled in.

 In 1936, Amy Johnson was the guest of honour at the opening of the first Butlin's holiday camp, at Ingoldmells, Skegness in 1936.

BILLY BUTLIN

The founder of the famous Butlin's Holiday camps, Billy Butlin, was born William Heygate Colborne Butlin in Cape Town in 1899, returning to England with his mother at the age of seven. For years he and his mother worked with his grandmother's fair around the country, before emigrating to Toronto, from where Butlin enlisted as a bugler in the Canadian Army and served in WWI. After the war he returned to England with just £5 in his pocket, most of which he invested in hiring a stall and travelling with his uncle's fair. Expanding to several stalls, he also secured a site at London's Olympia, eventually owning his own travelling fair.

In 1927 he opened a static fairground at Skegness, expanding it to include accommodation and opening his first holiday camp there in 1936. Two years later he created a second holiday camp at Clacton with other camps following after WWII at Filey, Ayr and Pwllheli and later at Mosney, Bognor Regis, Minehead and Barry Island. In 1959 he was surprised on his wedding day by Eamonn Andrews, for the TV programme *This is Your Life*. He was knighted in 1964.

Sir Billy Butlin was, after a fashion, responsible for the formation of Status Quo. The seeds of the group were planted at Butlin's Minehead when Rick Parfitt, playing there with The Highlights, met Francis Rossi, performing there with his group The Spectres; the latter featuring future Quo members Alan Lancaster and John Coghlan.

RICK PARFITT
& STATUS QUO

Status Quo first charted in 1968 with *Pictures of Matchstick Men*, a song Frances Rossi wrote in the toilet, where he'd gone for some peace and quiet and to get away from the family.

The group went on to have 64 hit singles, including 22 Top Ten hits, 32 hit albums, and a record-breaking 106 appearances on *Top of the Pops*. Many of their singles have become enduring classics, including as *Whatever You Want*, *Down Down*, *Caroline*, *Marguerita Time*, *Living on an Island*, *In the Army Now* and *Rockin' All Over the World*.

They opened Live Aid with the latter song in July 1985, and in 1991 won a Brit Award for Outstanding Contribution to Music. The band saw many personnel changes over the years, with only Francis Rossi and Rick Parfitt staying the course. Rick Parfitt died in 2016, and was commemorated the following year with a blue plaque in the centre of his home town of Woking, unveiled by his musician son, Richard.

At the unveiling of the plaque,

Richard said: 'Dad was never the sort of person to be comfortable with celebrity status. He was always part of what he considered to be a working man's band. He started off here in the working men's clubs; wherever he was in the world, he'd always make time to come back here. For me this is quite emotional. He would have been so embarrassed to be honoured by something like this… It means a lot to me, and he's probably looking down now going 'Yes!"

If one can credit Billy Butlin with have played a part in the formation of Status Quo, then surely the artist L.S. Lowry must also be acknowledged, as that song, **Pictures of Matchstick Men**, written by Francis Rossi in the smallest room, was a tribute to Lowry and kick-started an incredible career. Quo's single Rain was in the chart the day that Lowry died in February 1976.

L. S. LOWRY

Laurence Stephen Lowry, born in 1887 in Stretford, lived and worked in the Pendlebury area for more than forty years, turning down a knighthood and several other honours along the way. Lowry's work gives an insight into an industrial Lancashire of yesterday, with numerous chimneys belching smoke, mills, factories, a few old red buses but rarely a car to be seen, football on a Saturday and row upon row of terraced houses.

A large collection of Lowry's works are on display at The Lowry art gallery at Salford Quays and in 2013 Tate Britain held an exhibition with his first solo exhibition outside the UK taking place in Nanjing, China, in 2014. He created 1,000 paintings and 8,000 drawings.

In 2011 Lowry's painting *The Football Match* sold for a record £5.6 million with his Piccadilly Circus also selling for the same price later that year. In 2014 his depiction of Station Approach, Manchester sold for £2.3 million three years later, the same year that a collection of his paintings went for £15 million. In 2015 his 1950 painting, of a father and his two sons sold at auction for £1.7 million. Amazing for a man who humbly claimed, 'I am not an artist. I am a man who paints.'

LAWRENCE STEPHEN LOWRY 1887 - 1976
The famous North Country artist L.S. Lowry lived here from 1948 until his death in 1976.
The paintings of Lowry document the lives of ordinary people in the industrial communities of the North West.

*Lowry's painting **The Football Match**, depicting Bolton Wanderers' old ground Burnden Park in 1953, sold for £5.6 million in 2011*
Back in 1881 Bolton played at Pikes Lane where they stayed for 14 years. Once of their key players at that time was Kenny Davenport.

KENNY DAVENPORT

James Kenyon 'Kenny' Davenport (1862-1908) has gone down in history for being the scorer of the first ever football league goal, netting at 3.47 pm on 8th September 1888, playing for Bolton Wanderers against Derby County. A plaque commemorating the event was erected in Bolton in 2016.

Davenport was born in Bolton in 1862 and joined the First Division side having started playing with local team Gilnow Rangers in 1883. He later played for Southport and was twice capped for England, in 1885 and 1890. Retiring as a player in 1893, he returned to Bolton Wanderers to coach the reserve team.

Davenport died in 1908, unaware of his place in football history.

KENNY DAVENPORT
(1862-1908).
PLAYING HERE AT PIKES LANE
GROUND FOR BOLTON WANDERERS.
SCORED THE FIRST EVER LEAGUE GOAL
AGAINST DERBY COUNTY
AT 3.47PM ON SATURDAY
8TH SEPTEMBER 1888

On the same day as Kenny Davenport's historic goal, 8th September 1888, and only a few hours before, the body of Annie Chapman was discovered in Hanbury Street, East London - another murder ascribed to the killer given the name 'Jack the Ripper'.

MARY ANN NICHOLS, CATHERINE EDDOWES & ELIZABETH STRIDE

The infamous Jack the Ripper killings involved female prostitutes who lived and worked in the slums of East London's Whitechapel area; the victims had their throats cut and some had internal organs removed. There was extensive newspaper coverage and police investigation as the body count rose to eleven by 1891, with five confidently being claimed as victims of the Ripper. The first woman considered to be a victim of the Ripper was 43-year-old Mary Ann 'Polly' Nichols who was found in Buck's Row (later Durward Street) on 31st August 1888. Annie Chapman was the second murder with a third coming three weeks later.

CATHERINE EDDOWES

ELIZABETH STRIDE

MARY ANN NICHOLS

On 30th September, the body of 44-year-old Swedish-born Elizabeth 'Long Liz' Stride was discovered at Dutfield's Yard, Berner Street (now renamed Henriques Street). Originally from Gothenburg, where she was registered as a prostitute, she moved to London to work in 1866, married a ship's carpenter, and after his death lived with a dock labourer. Dr. Barnardo, another blue plaque recipient, had encountered the victim four days before her death.

Less than an hour after the discovery of Liz Stride there was another victim, 46-year-old Wolverhampton-born Catherine Eddowes, who was found in Mitre Square. She'd been taken into custody some hours earlier when she'd given a false name and address and was last seen alive at 1.35 am. 25-year-old Mary Jane Kelly, also known as Marie Jeanette Kelly (following a liaison with a French client), Fair Emma and Black Mary, may well have been the final victim of the Ripper. Her body was discovered in Miller's Court, Dorset Street, Spitalfields. Kelly claimed to have been born in Ireland before moving to Wales and then London, where she, like the other victims worked as a prostitute.

Kelly's body was far more extensively mutilated than the other, leading some historians to question whether this murder, which took place five weeks after the others, was indeed by the same hand. The five mentioned here are those that police, at the time, suggested were most likely to be linked.

The rumours and suggestions as to the identity of the serial killer continue unabated, and interest in the subject remains undimmed. There are blue plaques commemorating these three victims of the Ripper.

CITY OF LONDON CEMETERY

Mary Ann Nichols

Died 31st August 1888

HERITAGE TRAIL

Annie Chapman, known to some as 'Dark Annie', had been in a fight with a fellow lodger over a man, a week before her death. She was killed at the back of 29, Hanbury Street, just a few doors down from the birthplace of Bud Flanagan eight years later.

BUD FLANAGAN

Flanagan's parents Wolf and Yetta Weintrop were Polish Jews who had to flee from Radom, where they had been married, to Lodz, to escape a pogrom. They decided to start a new life in America, but a ticket agent cheated them and they discovered their ticket was for London.

Wolf, a shoemaker and part-time singer, settled his ever-growing family first in Brick Lane, then in Hanbury Street where their son Chaim Reuben Weintrop was born in 1896. He made his stage debut at the age of 12 at the London Music Hall, Shoreditch. Aged 14, keen to see something of the world, he walked from London to Southampton and blagged his way on to a ship, claiming to be a 17-year-old electrician.

In New York he jumped ship and worked for Western Union and on a North Dakota farm, before joining a Vaudeville show and touring the USA. He then sailed with them to perform in New Zealand, Australia and South Africa. Back in San Francisco, he decided to return to England to fight for his country in WWI, joining the Royal Field Artillery as Robert Weintrop. He served with the unpopular Sergeant Major Flanagan, whose name he took on forming a comedy double act, Flanagan and Roy, in 1919.

The most endearing and enduring double act he would form would be with Chesney Allen, the pair having met during WWI in Flanders; they didn't work together, however, until 1925. Their mix of music and comedy led to a recording career and the pair worked in tandem as part of the world-famous troupe, The Crazy Gang.

Although Allen wasn't a singer, and tended to speak the lines behind Bud Flanagan, they made many songs their own in a very chummy, homespun way. Three of the most popular were the WWII classic *We're Going To Hang Out The Washing On The Siegfried Line*, *Run Rabbit Run*, and *Underneath the Arches*, which Flanagan co-wrote.

After Chesney Allen retired in 1945, Flanagan continued with a solo career as well as working with the Crazy Gang. He was awarded the OBE in 1959 and he was a proud member of the Grand Order of Water Rats.

Bud Flanagan died in 1968. His legacy not only includes music and laughter, but also the Bud Flanagan Leukaemia Fund.

*The last song Bud Flanagan recorded, shortly before his death in 1968, was **Who Do You Think You Are Kidding, Mr. Hitler?**, which was used as the theme to the popular TV series **Dad's Army**, starring Arthur Lowe as the arrogant Captain Mainwaring.*

ARTHUR LOWE

Born in 1915 in Hayford, Derbyshire, Lowe began his career in the theatre just before WWII but it wasn't until the first half of the 1960s that he became a familiar face on television through the role of Leonard Swindley in *Coronation Street*.

The *Dad's Army* series ran from 1968 to 1977 with Arthur Lowe playing the bumptious, postulating and pompous Captain Mainwaring against John le Mesurier's Sergeant Wilson. Although best known for his role in *Dad's Army*, which also spawned a film in 1971, Lowe also appeared in plays at the National Theatre and Royal Court Theatre and was invited by fellow blue plaque recipient Sir Laurence Olivier to act at the Old Vic. He also appeared in *The Tempest* alongside Sir John Gielgud.

He continued with the role on the spin-off series' *Pardon the Expression* in 1966 and *Turn out the Lights* in 1967, but he was keen to move away from playing the same character. Arthur Lowe continued to appear on the stage and had

been seen in such TV series as *Z Cars* and *The Avengers*, before landing the role of Captain Mainwaring. He was nominated for seven BAFTAs but was dogged by ill-health in later years. He died in 1982, aged sixty-six.

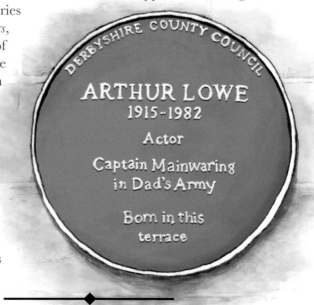

His London blue plaque is on his house in Maida Vale, overlooking the Regent's Canal.

Walmington-on-Sea's Home Guard might have been fiction, but in Ilkley the Home Guard met and trained in a drill hall built three years before WWI for the Territorials 4th West Riding Brigade. They share the honours on their blue plaque.

THE DRILL HALL, ILKLEY

The Drill Hall, Ilkey was completed in September 1911, just before the Coronation of George V and a visit to England by the Kaiser. The hall not only had stabling for the horses but also living quarters for non-commissioned officers, officers' quarters and a bar.

At the start of WWI in 1914, the commanding officer led 127 local volunteers into action and they went off to war again in 1939, having become the 11th Howitzers. During WWII, the hall became the headquarters of the Home Guard. It ceased to be used by the military in 1970, since which time the building has been used for business purposes.

Since Remembrance Day 2012, the plaque has been 'Guarding the Home Guard's Home', echoing George Formby's song of the same name.

GEORGE FORMBY

Born George Hoy Booth in Wigan, Lancashire in 1904, George Formby took his stage moniker from his father, who had performed under that name. After spells as a stable boy and a jockey, he took to the stage after the death of his father in 1921, taking over the same jokes, songs and characters.

In 1923 he bought a ukulele and married Beryl Ingham, both of which would set him on the path to becoming the UK's highest-paid entertainer. Beryl changed his act, insisting that the ukulele be a permanent part of it, and that he dressed formally. Formby started his recording career in 1927 and at one point was releasing a song almost every month.

He also became an incredibly successful comedy film star, playing a gormless character with his high-pitched voice, naïvety, cheeky grin, infectious giggle and his catchphrase 'Turned out nice again'. During WWII, Formby did many shows for ENSA (Entertainments National Service Association), entertaining the troops, appearing in front of some 3 million service personnel in 16 countries during the conflict.

Like Bud Flanagan and Chesney Allen, he also made a successful recording of *We're Going to Hang Out The Washing on the Siegfried Line*, as well as popular songs *Leaning on a Lamp Post*, *When I'm Cleaning Windows*, *Bless 'Em All*, and *Chinese Laundry Blues*. In 1951 he starred in the West End musical *Zip Goes a Million*.

Formby's biographer considered that the actor 'had been able to embody simultaneously Lancashire, the working classes, the people, and the nation.'

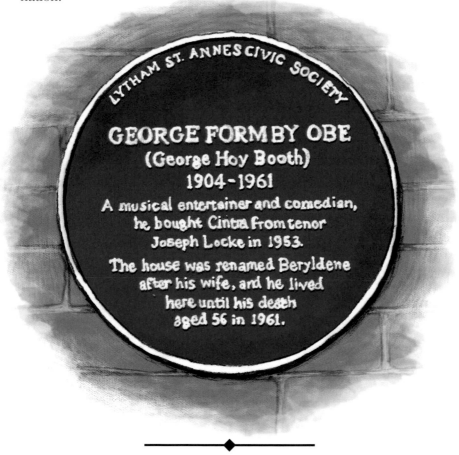

GEORGE FORMBY OBE
(George Hoy Booth)
1904-1961
A musical entertainer and comedian,
he bought Cintra from tenor
Joseph Locke in 1953.
The house was renamed Beryldene
after his wife, and he lived
here until his death
aged 56 in 1961.

There is a plaque at the Midland Hotel in Bradford commemorating Formby's stay there whilst performing at the Alhambra in 1940. Thirty-five years earlier, the actor Henry Irving had died on the main staircase at that same hotel.

HENRY IRVING

Sir Henry Irving was born John Henry Broadribb in 1838 and became a giant of the theatrical world as an actor-manager, producing many successful shows at London's Lyceum theatre. In 1878, Irving formed a partnership with the eminent actress Dame Ellen Terry, opening the Lyceum under his own management and reviving *Hamlet*, *Othello*, *Romeo and Juliet*, *The Merchant of Venice*, *Much Ado About Nothing*, *Twelfth Night*, *King Lear* and many more.

Irving also took his Lyceum Company on successful tours of the United States and Canada. Henry Irving was the first actor to receive a knighthood, giving a nod to the increasingly respectability of the stage as a career.

Irving was the main inspiration for the title character of Bram Stoker's 1897 novel. **Dracula**. *Stoker was Henry Irving's business manager, and was with him when the great actor died in 1905, at the Midland Hotel, Bradford.*

BRAM STOKER

Bram Stoker, born Abraham Stoker in 1847, idolised Henry Irving, and worked as his personal assistant and business manager from 1878. As one biographer observed, Stoker's friendship with Irving was 'the most important love relationship of his adult life'.

Historian Louis S. Warren declared that 'scholars have long agreed that keys to Dracula's tale's origin and meaning lie in the manager's relationship with Irving in the 1880s… Stoker's numerous descriptions of Irving correspond so closely to his rendering of the fictional count that contemporaries commented on the resemblance… But Bram Stoker also internalized the fear and animosity his employed inspired in him, making them the foundation for his gothic fiction'.

Another contributory factor to Stoker's version of *Dracula* was almost certainly him meeting Hungarian writer Armin Vambery, who regaled him with dark tales of the Carpathian Mountains, initiating Stoker's research into stories of vampires. Whilst Stoker may have borrowed the name of his central character from Vlad III Dracula, it's unlikely that he based the character on him.

In 1906, a year after Irving's death, Bram Stoker published a biography about his employer, *Personal Reminiscences of Henry Irving*. Stoker also wrote for the *Daily Telegraph* and produced plays for the Prince of Wales Theatre. Many regard Stoker as a repressed homosexual who used fiction as an outlet for his frustrations. He began writing *Dracula* just weeks after the conviction of his friend and fellow blue plaque recipient, Oscar Wilde. In 1912, Stoker demanded that all homosexual authors be imprisoned, which some historians put down to his own self-loathing.

The original manuscript of Stoker's book went missing, and was presumed lost until being re-discovered in a barn in Pennsylvania, whose founder now also has a blue plaque. The typescript consisted of 541 pages, with the front page having the handwritten title, *THE UN-DEAD*. The title was changed to *Dracula* just before publication.

 Dracula *is now regarded as one of the two great creations of gothic horror, alongside Mary Shelley's* **Frankenstein**.

MARY SHELLEY

Mary Shelley was born Mary Wollstonecraft Godwin in 1797, in Somers Town, London. Her mother died a month after giving birth to her, resulting in Mary being brought up by her father, the political philosopher William Godwin. In 1814 she began a romance with one of her father's political followers, the poet Percy Bysshe Shelley, despite the fact that he was married.

She travelled through Europe with Shelley and her stepsister, Claire Clairmont, who would have a child by their friend Lord Byron, as Mary fell pregnant by Shelley.

Mary and Percy struggled with debt, the death of their daughter and the suicide of Shelley's wife, but they married in 1816, spending that summer with Byron and Claire Clairmont near Geneva.

It was there that, following a challenge to see who could write the best horror story, she conceived the idea for *Frankenstein*. From 1817 the Shelleys lived at Marlow, where they were visited by Lord Byron.

They left for Italy in 1818 where Mary gave birth to their only surviving child. In 1822, Percy Shelley drowned after his boat sank during a storm near Viareggio. Mary Shelley returned to England the following year and spent the rest of her life raising her son and working as an author.

Valperga was published in 1823, *Perkin Warbeck* in 1830, *The Last Man* in 1826, *Lodore* in 1835, and *Falkner* in 1837. She also edited the works of her husband. Mary Shelley died of a brain tumour in 1851 at Chester Square, London. Her best-known work is undoubtedly *Frankenstein: or, The Modern Prometheus*.

ENGLISH HERITAGE

MARY SHELLEY
1797-1851
Author of
Frankenstein
lived here
1846-1851

Before moving to Marlow, the Shelleys lived at 87, Marchmont Street; well over 100 years later actor, and comedian Kenneth Williams lived at no. 57.

KENNETH WILLIAMS

Born in 1926, Kenneth Williams grew up in London. He joined the Royal Engineers during WWII, where he first considered being an entertainer. After cutting his teeth in repertory theatre from 1948, he landed a plum job in the radio series *Hancock's Half Hour*, after the radio producer Denis Main Wilson saw him in Bernard Shaw's *St. Joan* in the West End in 1954.

In *Hancock's Half Hour*, Williams would appear as assorted characters, the audience clearly adoring it when he popped up with his slightly nasal, camp voice, with such lines as 'good evening' and 'stop messin' about'. He appeared in the entire run of the radio series, as well as continuing to appear on stage in such plays as Orson Welles' *Moby Dick*. Williams fell out with Welles, as he did with many people, due to his irascible nature, coupled with his finding it difficult to come to terms with his homosexuality and recurring depression.

He appeared in twenty-six of the thirty-one *Carry On* films (for just £5,000 a time) as well as moving to the radio series *Beyond Our Ken* (1858-64) and the sequel, *Round the Horne* (1965-68). He took a variety of roles in the latter series, including that of folk singer Rambling Syd Rumpo, the sleazy J. Peasemold Gruntfuttock, and Sandy, one half of Julian and Sandy, the camp couple who rather daringly talked the homosexual argot, Polari.

Williams appeared in many West End revues and was a regular, if cantankerous and argumentative, panelist on the radio show *Just A Minute* for twenty years. He was also a regular reader on the children's TV series *Jackanory* and the voice of the cartoon characters in the TV series *Willo the Wisp*.

On the topic of blue plaques, Williams had once remarked to a well-known actress, whilst walking down the street and catching sight of a plaque, 'Oh, I never want one of them things.' He died of an overdose in 1988, and now 'one of them things' commemorates him.

Tony Hancock, the comedian whose series launched Williams' career, is also a blue plaque recipient.

TONY HANCOCK

Tony Hancock was born in Birmingham but raised in Bournemouth, where a plaque on his childhood home mentions his first professional engagement.

The radio series *Hancock's Half Hour* began broadcasting on the BBC in 1954 and on television from 1956, written by Ray Galton and Alan Simpson. The radio series included Sid James, Kenneth Williams and Bill Kerr, with Moira Lister and then Andrée Melly playing Hancock's 'girlfriend'. It was set around the house of 'Anthony Aloysius St John Hancock' at the fictitious 23, Railway Cuttings, East Cheam. Hattie Jacques later became a fixture of the cast as Griselda 'Grisly' Pugh.

The TV series was initially more of a double act between Hancock and Sid James, which troubled Hancock to such an extent that he announced in 1960 that he would plough his own furrow and go solo. He was the first performer to command £1,000 for a half-hour show, pulling in massive audiences, and he became one of Britain's biggest stars of the era.

Many episodes of his programmes have become enduring classics, such as *The Blood Donor, Sunday Afternoon at Home, The Wild Man of the Woods, The Radio Ham*, and *The Bowmans,* (a spoof of *The Archers*). Hancock later split with Galton and Simpson, after which his career declined.

Hancock also made a handful of films, including *The Artist* and *The Punch and Judy Man*, the latter shot on location in Bognor Regis with Hugh Lloyd, who often had cameos in Hancock's later TV series.

 Tony Hancock was just forty-four years old when he committed suicide in an Australian hotel in June 1968.

Tony Hancock was born in Birmingham, where the author J.R.R. Tolkien spent his formative years and who has also been honoured with a blue plaque.

J. R. R. TOLKIEN

As a boy, John Ronald Reul Tolkien lived just 300 yards from Sarehole Mill, a Grade II listed water mill on the River Cole. He would use the location as the Mill at Hobbiton in his book *The Lord of the Rings*.
'It was a kind of lost paradise. There was an old mill that really did grind corn with two millers, a great big pond with swans on it, a wonderful dell with flowers, a few old-fashioned village houses...'

The grounds now host the annual Tolkien Weekend, celebrating his life and works. Tolkien, born 1892, is best known as the author of *The Hobbit*, written in the 1930s, and *The Lord of the Rings*, both based in his imaginary world of Middle Earth, the latter book written in the first half of the 1950s.

As Rawlinson and Bosworth Professor of Anglo-Saxon, his knowledge of the subject undoubtedly helped in his construction of the world, language, characters and environment of both *The Hobbit* and the three books that comprise *The Lord of the Rings*. Tolkien was also a Fellow of Pembroke College, Oxford from 1925-1945 and Merton Professor of English Language and Literature, and Fellow of Merton College from 1945-1959.

The Times ranked him 6th on a list of 'The 50 greatest British writers since 1945'. Tolkien was awarded the CBE in 1972, his son Christopher overseeing the publishing of *The Silmarillion* after his father's death in 1973. *The Lord of the Rings* has sold in the region of 150 million copies to date, with *The Hobbit* selling 100 million.

Tolkien's books remain wildly popular and spawned countless imitators and homages under the umbrella of 'fantasy' fiction. *The Lord of the Rings* has been adapted several times for radio, film, comics and videogames, with Ralph Baskshi's animated version being the first to reach the big screen in 1978, and Peter Jackson's trilogy of movies launching in 2001; the first of the prequel films based on *The Hobbit* was released in 2012.

In a letter to the publisher Raynor Unwin, of George Allen & Unwin, on 13th May 1954, Tolkien wrote about a spat with Geoffrey Mure the warden, mentioning another Oxford man:

'He went so far as to say that Merton seemed to be doing well though he doubted if I should quite get into the Roger Bannister class'.

A week earlier, Roger Bannister had become the first person to run a sub-four-minute mile, with the help of pacemakers Chris Chataway and Chris Brasher. The hero of the hour, like Tolkien, was at Merton College at the time of the world record.

ROGER BANNISTER

Born in Harrow in 1929, Roger Bannister attended University College, London, the University of Oxford (Exeter College and Merton College) and St Mary's Hospital Medical School. His inspiration on the athletics track had been Sydney Wooderson, the slight, bespectacled runner and one-mile record holder. It was assumed that if anyone could break the four-minute mile it was most likely to be Wooderson, who had already run it in 4:04.2.

Bannister however was the man to accomplish it; the record was set on 6th May, 1954 at the Iffley Road track at Oxford.

A distinguished neurologist, Roger Bannister was knighted in 1975 and became Master of Pembroke College, retiring in 1993. He died on 3 March, 2018.

———————◆———————

Another fellow of Pembroke College, Oxford was James Smithson, the founder of the Smithsonian Institute.

JAMES SMITHSON

Born around 1765, James Smithson was the illegitimate son of the 1st Duke of Northumberland. After a clandestine birth in Paris, he was christened Jacques-Louis Macie, later amended to James Louis.

He was naturalised in England and studied chemistry and mineralogy at Pembroke College, Oxford. At the age of 22 he changed his name from Macie to his father's pre-marriage surname, Smithson. Unmarried, he left his estate to his nephew, with the caveat that were his nephew to die without heirs that his estate be used 'to found in Washington, under the name of the Smithsonian Institution, an establishment for the increase and diffusion of knowledge among men.'

When his nephew died childless in 1835, Smithson's estate passed to the United States of America to found the Smithsonian Institution in Washington DC, even though the benefactor had never visited the United States. President Andrew Jackson sent US diplomat Richard Rush to collect the money, Rush returning to the States with 105 sacks containing around $500,000 worth of gold sovereigns, worth about $11,500,000 today. Despite Smithson's mandate being fairly vague, ex-President John Quincey Adams persuaded his country to use the money for the purposes it was intended, so in 1846, eight years after the money had been collected, President James K. Polk signed the legislation that established the Smithsonian Institution, a group of museums and research centres that holds some 154 million items and is visited by 30 million people a year. The Institution even has its own blue and yellow flag.

His father was born Hugh Smithson in 1712 and inherited the Smithson Baronetcy in 1733, but changed his name to Percy on marrying Lady Elizabeth Seymour, the daughter of the 7th Duke of Somerset. Elizabeth was also Baroness Percy in her own right, and indirect heiress of the Percy family who had previously held the Earldom of Northumberland. The title of Earl of Northumberland passed by special remainder to Hugh Percy, as Elizabeth's husband, when her father died. Hugh was created 1st Duke of Northumberland in 1788, Baron Lovaine in 1794. He had two sons and a daughter by his wife and the later styled James Smithson by Elizabeth

Hungerford Keate. His central London seat, Northumberland House was demolished to enable the creation of Trafalgar Square.

His other properties included Syon House, Alnwick Castle, Kielder Castle and Stanwick Hall. He was a patron of Canaletto, acquiring two of his large paintings, and was one of the commissioners for Westminster Bridge. The family owned Northumberland.

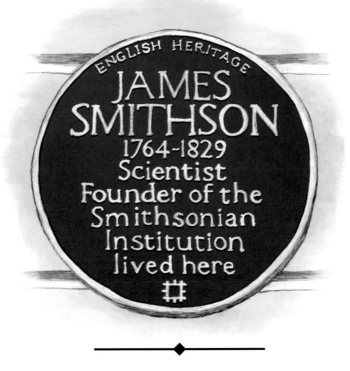

The family also occupied an ancient house and land at Tottenham High Cross in London, now long demolished; Northumberland Row was built on the site. Percy House High Road N17 was built by Hugh Smithson between 1745 and 1750, before he became Hugh Percy.

Tottenham's ground, Northumberland Park, was part of the estate of Henry Percy, alias Harry Hotspur, as made famous by Shakespeare in Henry IV, which led them to use the name 'Hotspur.' Their captain in the 1960-61 season, Danny Blanchflower, has often been cited as the club's best ever player.

DANNY BLANCHFLOWER

Robert Dennis 'Danny' Blanchflower was born in Belfast in 1926. He signed for Glentoran FC in 1946, before moving to Barnsley for £6,000 three years later. In 1951, he went to Aston Villa for £15,000 and made 155 appearances for the club before being sold to Tottenham Hotspur during the 1954-55 season, for £30,000.

He'd made his debut as a Northern Ireland International in 1949, earning 56 caps for his country, and in 1958 helped them reach the quarter-finals of the World Cup. He made 382 appearances during his ten years with the club, and in 1960-61 captained the side that won the both the League and the FA Cup, making Hotspur the first team in the 20th century to complete the double.

He was voted Footballer of the Year in 1958 and again in 1961. He scored a penalty in the 1962 FA Cup Final, which Spurs won, and the

following year captained the side to victory over Atlético Madrid to win the European Cup Winner's Cup. During his time with Spurs, Blanchflower also played for Toronto City alongside fellow legends Stanley Matthews and Johnny Haynes.

He's responsible for one of the best known quotes about football: 'The great fallacy is that the game is first and last about winning. It is nothing of the kind. The game is about glory, it is about doing things in style and with a flourish, about going out and beating the lot, not waiting for them to die of boredom.'

He retired as a player in 1964 at the age of 38, having played nearly 400 games in all competitions for Spurs and captaining them to win four major trophies, going on to manage Northern Ireland and Chelsea.

A plaque was unveiled in 2015 by his daughters, and goalkeeper Pat Jennings, at their father's childhood home in Grace Avenue, Belfast.

Away from football, Blanchflower became a familiar face on television through featuring in a Shredded Wheat commercial, famously saying, 'Pass the hot milk please.'

Another international footballer, Brian Clough, also appeared in TV advertisements for Shredded Wheat. The then Nottingham Forest Manager starred in four Shredded Wheat TV Commercials during 1991 and 1992, with cameos from England players Gary Lineker, Peter Shilton, and Bryan Robson.

A decade earlier, Clough had also endorsed Bran Crunchies in an earlier TV commercial.

BRIAN CLOUGH

Born in 1935, Brian Clough was a footballer of great renown. The high-scoring forward played for Middlesbrough and Sunderland, and was twice capped for England in 1959. Injury brought his playing career to an end at the age of twenty-nine.

The fact that he didn't manage the national side means he is often referred to as 'the greatest manager England never had'. He did, however, manage Hartlepool United from 1965, Derby County from 1967, Brighton & Hove Albion from 1973, Leeds United from 1974, and Nottingham Forest from 1975-1993. Apart from his short term with Leeds (44 days), Clough's assistant manager had been the ever-present Peter Taylor. Clough took Forest into the old First Division, winning the title the following season, for the first time in the club's history. His team also won two consecutive European Cups and two League Cups.

After Taylor retired in 1982, Clough stayed on for another ten years, winning two more League Cups, and took Forest into the 1991 FA Cup Final. After Forest were relegated in 1993, Clough retired from football. Always outspoken, sometimes controversial, usually opinionated, the charismatic Clough was often blunt and to the point.

MIDDLESBROUGH'S HERITAGE

International Footballer and Football Manager
BRIAN CLOUGH
was born here on
21st March 1935
He was associated with
Middlesbrough Football Club
at Ayresome Park
from 1951 to 1961

*Brian Clough was born in 1935. The bestselling song that year was **Cheek to Cheek**, written by Irving Berlin for the Fred Astaire and Ginger Rogers film **Top Hat**, sung by Astaire himself. Astaire also has a blue plaque, in Lismore.*

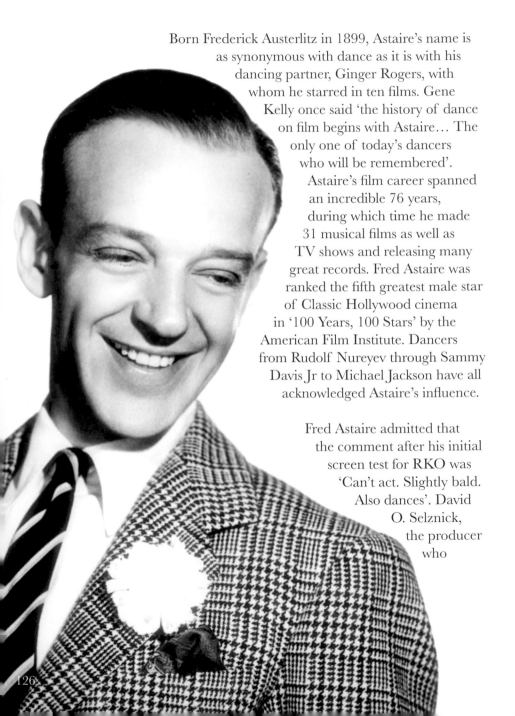

FRED ASTAIRE

Born Frederick Austerlitz in 1899, Astaire's name is as synonymous with dance as it is with his dancing partner, Ginger Rogers, with whom he starred in ten films. Gene Kelly once said 'the history of dance on film begins with Astaire… The only one of today's dancers who will be remembered'. Astaire's film career spanned an incredible 76 years, during which time he made 31 musical films as well as TV shows and releasing many great records. Fred Astaire was ranked the fifth greatest male star of Classic Hollywood cinema in '100 Years, 100 Stars' by the American Film Institute. Dancers from Rudolf Nureyev through Sammy Davis Jr to Michael Jackson have all acknowledged Astaire's influence.

Fred Astaire admitted that the comment after his initial screen test for RKO was 'Can't act. Slightly bald. Also dances'. David O. Selznick, the producer who commissioned the screen test commented, 'I am uncertain about the man, but I feel, in spite of his enormous ears and bad chin line, that his charm is so tremendous that it comes through even on this wretched test'.

Astaire was wary of being part of another pairing, having danced with his sister, but the partnership with Ginger Rogers proved enduring and popular.

A plaque to Fred Astaire was unveiled on Main Street, Lismore, Co. Waterford in 2000 by Fred's daughter, Ava Astaire McKenzie, in recognition of his link to the village, having visited his sister Adele at her home, Lismore Castle, from the mid-1930s until his death in 1987. Fred and Adele danced together until 1932 when she married Lord Charles Cavendish, the second son of the 9th Duke of Devonshire.

*When Adele Astaire's husband died in 1944, she refused an offer to return to the stage in **Annie Get Your Gun**, but it wasn't the first time she'd turned down a major role. When she'd been a young girl, J.M. Barrie had asked her to play the first Wendy in **Peter Pan**, but she had to excuse herself for contractual reasons. Barrie himself has a clutch of blue plaques.*

J. M. BARRIE

Scottish novelist Sir James Matthew Barrie, 1st Baronet, OM was born in 1860. His father was a weaver and the family were extremely poor. When Barrie found commercial success as an author, he would become a well-known and very wealthy celebrity, and a very generous one at that.

When he moved to London, he was inspired to write stories after meeting Daphne du Maurier's cousins, the Llewelyn Davis boys, Peter, Michael, Jack, George and Nicholas. Not only were they the inspiration for *Peter Pan*, but Barrie also became their guardian after the death of their parents.

The enduring story of Peter Pan, and Neverland, with a cast that included Wendy, Michael and John, the Darling children, their dog Nana, the Lost Boys, Captain Hook and Smee, was first staged in the early 1900s. It has captivated generations of children and adults alike, including Michael Jackson, who called his house Neverland, claiming 'I am Peter Pan. He represents youth, childhood, never growing up, magic, flying'.

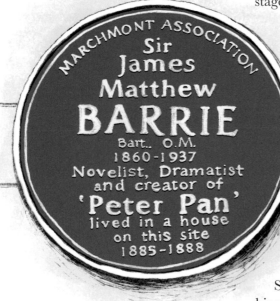

In 1922, Barrie generously left the rights to *Peter Pan* in perpetuity to the Great Ormond Street Children's Hospital in his will.

◆

In the 1880s, Ormond Street and new Ormond Street were merged into Great Ormond Street. As well as generations of children, another one-time resident of Great Ormond Street was the first English prison reformer John Howard.

128

JOHN HOWARD

John Howard was born in 1728, in North London. Howard's father was a wealthy upholsterer with property at Cardington, Bedfordshire, where the boy was sent to live after the death of his mother. He was left a large inheritance in his father's will, and subsequently toured the continent, becoming ill on returning to London. He was nursed back to health by Sarah Loidore, thirty years his senior; he married her, but she herself died just three years later.

After setting off for Portugal in 1755, he was captured and imprisoned by French privateers. After a few days in gaol he was exchanged for a French officer held by the British. It's thought that his subsequent meeting with the Commissioners of Sick and Wounded Seamen on behalf of fellow captives sparked his interest in prison reform.

He returned to live in Cardington, on a 200-acre estate, part of which he'd inherited from his grandparents, his grandmother being related to the Whitbread family. Always philanthropic, he paid for the 23 local children to be educated and was always looking to improve the lives of his tenants. In 1773 he was elected High Sherrif of Bedfordshire, and having inspected the county prison he was moved to examine prison conditions in several hundred jails across the country.

He addressed a House of Commons select committee on the subject and published the first edition of *The State of the Prisons* in 1777. His proposals and recommendations to improve the mental and physical state of prisoners were once again put to the House of Commons, with Howard having travelled some 42,000 miles in pursuit of his suggestions for prison reform.

In 1787 he published *The State of the Prisons in England*, and *An Account of the Principal Lazarettos of Europe*. After his death from typhus, following a prison visit in the Ukraine, he became the first civilian to be honoured with a statue in St Paul's Cathedral, with other statues in Bedford and Kherson.

Almost 80 years after his death, The Howard Association was formed with the aim of 'promotion of the most efficient means of penal treatment and crime prevention'. In 1921 the Association merged with the Penal Reform league to become the Howard League for Penal Reform, which remains Britain's biggest penal reform organisation to the present day.

 As well as being the home of John Howard, Cardington was also the base for airship builders, the Short Brothers. The Cardington Airship Factory displays a plaque to that effect.

THE SHORT BROTHERS

The Short Brothers were Horace (1872-1917) Eustace (1875-1932) and Oswald (1883-1969), with Oswald being the driving force behind their aeronautical engineering company.

They established the firm's seaplane factory at Rochester in 1914 and their airship factory at Cardington in 1916, with Oswald as the chairman of the firm from 1919, becoming managing director in 1932. His pioneering work on 'stressed skin' aircraft construction gained global acceptance. The Short Brothers HQ at Cardington became The Royal Airship Works from 1924-1938 where the airship R101 was constructed.

The craft's first flight, on 14th October 1929, lasted almost 6 hours. The following flights increased in duration, and its seventh outing lasted over 30 hours. After more flights and trials, on 4th October 1930, the R101 left Cardington for Karachi, India but came down in France, near Allonne, resulting in 48 of the 54 passengers losing their lives.

Airship R100 had been built by the Airship Guarantee Company, a subsidiary of Vickers-Armstrong, with a design team lead by Barnes

Wallis. It undertook its first flight in December 1929, from the airship's base in Howden to Cardington, and made a successful crossing of the Atlantic from there at the end of July 1930. The airship reached the docking base outside Montreal in 78 hours, remained for twelve days and returned successfully to Cardington in just 57 and a half hours.

It seemed as though airships may be a great part of the future transport system, but it was not to be. Following the success of the R100, the R101 team were determined not to be beaten and were adamant that they could reach India, but R101 engineers and colleagues of Barnes Wallis felt that the R100 was a superior ship. After the R101 disaster, R100 was broken up for scrap.

However, the company that the Short brothers formed remained a significant and influential manufacturer of aircraft, long after the brothers' own involvement with it ended. It became famed for turning out brilliant aeronautical engineers.

TRANSPORT TRUST

THE SHORTS
BUILDING 1917

Headquarters of Short Brothers (1917-1921)
and the Royal Airship Works (1924-1928)
where HM Airship R101 was designed

For further information visit
www.transportheritage.com

TRANSPORT HERITAGE SITE

A red, rather than blue, plaque adorns the building where the company first had its headquarters in Cardington, Bedfordshire.

Barnes Wallis was chief engineer of the R100 project, and would go on to have an even greater role to play in the history of aernautical engineering..

BARNES WALLIS

Sir Barnes Wallis was an airship designer, as well as designing the Swing Wing and most famously 'the bouncing bomb,' that would, in the hands of 617 Squadron, destroy the Ruhr dams, the Mohne, Eder, and Sorpe.

The Air Ministry had been discussing the massive disruption the breaching of these dams would cause, for some time, but it was Barnes Wallis who came up with his invention that made the idea a success. The idea had initially been inspired by a football skimming across a wet pitch while he was watching Millwall play.

After their home ground, the Den, was bombed in 1941, Barnes Wallis was determined to make the enemy compensate for the damage.

There are countless memorials to Barnes Wallis, including a statue in Herne Bay, a display in the Yorkshire Air Museum, and public houses named after him in Howden in Yorkshire, and Ripley in Derbyshire.

TRANSPORT TRUST

SIR BARNES N. WALLIS
(1887-1979)

Aeronautical Engineer and Inventor, designer of airships, aeroplanes, the 'Bouncing Bomb' and swing-wing aircraft, was born here.

For further information visit
www.transportheritage.com

TRANSPORT HERITAGE SITE

*Barnes Wallis was also immortalised on film, portrayed by Michael Redgrave in the classic movie **The Dambusters**, which told the story of the raid. The evocative and memorable theme tune was written by the king of light orchestral music, Eric Coates.*

ERIC COATES

Born in 1886, Eric Coates later studied at the Royal Academy of Music and played viola in the Queen's Hall Orchestra under Henry Wood.
Eric Coates was one of the most successful of the light classical composers, some of his most popular pieces being *Calling All Workers*, the theme for the radio series *Music While You Work*, *The Knightsbridge March* (from the London Suite) which became the theme for the radio and TV series *In Town Tonigh*t, *The Dambusters March*, and *By the Sleepy Lagoon* - the theme for the long-running radio series *Desert Island Discs*. He also wrote *Halcyon Days*, used as the theme for the TV series *The Forsyte Saga*, and *Music Everywhere*, which became *The Rediffusion March* for Associated-Rediffusion Television.

He occasionally worked with a rather unusual lyricist in fellow plaque recipient Arthur Conan Doyle, as well as Fred Weatherly, who wrote the words for *Danny Boy*.

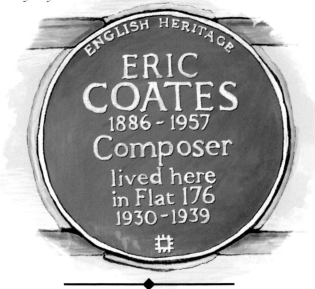

 *When **Desert Island Discs** started, the BBC was just twenty years old. The BBC's first Director General, and the person who founded it, was John (later Lord) Reith.*

JOHN REITH

John Charles Walsham Reith was born on 20th July 1889 at Stonehaven, Kincardineshire. His family lived in Glasgow at the time, but were holidaying when his mother went into labour. His father was a minister, and John saw little of him as he was growing up. In 1914 he left home for London and shortly became a dock worker, until the First World War sent him to the front lines, where he was shot in the cheek in 1915, having been made a lieutenant earlier in the year. He transferred to the Royal Engineers and became a captain, eventually resigning his commission in 1921.

After a stint in business and politics, he applied for the job of Director General of the yet to be established British Broadcasting Corporation. He got the job, and his direction for the fledgling enterprise was crucial. In the groundbreaking work he carried out in forming the BBC, he compared himself to the founder of the printing press, William Caxton.

ENGLISH HERITAGE

LORD REITH
1889–1971
First Director-General of the BBC
lived here
1924–1930

Lord Reith's guiding mantra for the BBC was that it should 'inform, educate and entertain' - in that order. He laid the groundwork for the BBC's original reputation for impartiality and quality programming.

◆

Just a few years after the birth of BBC radio came BBC television, thanks to the innovative and groundbreaking work of John Logie Baird.

JOHN LOGIE BAIRD

John Logie Baird was born in Helensburgh, Scotland in 1888. He graduated from the Royal Technical College in Glasgow, now Strathclyde University. His experiments led to him transmitting the image of a Maltese Cross over a distance of ten feet, in 1924. In March 1925, Baird demonstrated his ideas with moving silhouettes over a three-week period at Selfridges store in London, and later that year successfully transmitted the first television picture with a ventriloquist's dummy, 'Stooky Bill'. He then brought 20-year-old office worker William Staynton, who worked downstairs, into the studio, and the lad became the first ever televised human face.

Baird felt that the public needed to be made aware of his invention, so to promote it he went to the *Daily Express*. On hearing there was a crazy guy on the premises making some ludicrous claims, the editor said to one of his reporters, 'For God's sake go down to reception and get rid of a lunatic who's down there. He says he's got a machine for seeing by wireless! Watch him. He may have a razor on him.'

John Logie Baird's first 'televisor', as he called it, was made from a hatbox, a tea chest, bicycle lights, a pair of scissors, sealing wax, and glue. Early in 1926, he repeated his transmissions for a reporter from *The Times* and scientists from the Royal Institute, in his laboratory at 22, Frith Street, Soho, London. Two days later *The Times* reported on Baird's invention and published the first known photograph of a televised human being, the inventor's business partner, Oliver Hutchinson.

By 1927, Baird's television was demonstrated over 438 miles of telephone line between London and Glasgow and he'd formed the Baird Television Development Company. Baird not only invented television, but surprisingly he invented colour television as well, making his breakthrough in the mid-1920s. In 1931, he televised the first live transmission of the Epsom Derby. Early in 1937, the BBC stopped using Baird's transmission method in favour of the EMI-Marconi system.

If John Logie Baird had been better at making jam, we might not have had television. In 1919, at the age of thirty-one, a few years before his experiments with vision, he sailed to Port of Spain in Trinidad where he set up a jam factory. With the island being rich in sugar cane and citrus fruits, he reasoned that his venture could do well. It didn't. It seemed that insects were attracted by the sugar and were giving the conserve extra body.

By the autumn of 1920, Logie Baird was back in Britain, but a then four year old called Claudia Jones, another inhabitant of Port of Spain, Trinidad, would go on to make her mark in an entirely different way.

CLAUDIA JONES

Claudia Jones was born Claudia Vera Cumberbatch in 1915, and in 1924 would move to New York City with her family at the age of nine. Ten years later, she joined the Young Communist League USA and began writing for *The Daily Worker*.

When the Communist League became the American Youth for Democracy Movement during WWII, she became the editor for its magazine. After the Great War, she became the executive secretary for the Woman's National Commission and secretary for the Women's Commission of the Communist Party USA. In 1952 Jones took the same position at the National Peace Council and a year later took over the editorship of Negro Affairs.

In 1948, her communist activities led to her being arrested and sentenced to the first of four prison terms, and at the end of 1950 she was ordered to be deported. She wasn't deported, but having been found guilty of 'un-American activities', she wasn't released from jail until 1955. She was refused entry to Trinidad and Tobago, but was offered residency in the United Kingdom on humanitarian grounds. On arrival she immediately became involved in the organisation of the British Afro-Caribbean community and the fight for equal rights.

Mentored by the singer Paul Robeson, she campaigned tirelessly against racism in employment, housing and education. She addressed peace rallies, the Trade Union Congress and spoke in Japan, Russia and China as well as campaigning for the release of Nelson Mandela. Jones founded *The West Indian Gazette* and Afro-Asian Caribbean News to help give black people a voice, and following the 1958 race riots in Notting Hill and Nottingham she spearheaded something longer lasting - The Notting Hill Carnival.

Jones used her connections to secure St Pancras Town Hall, where in January 1959, the first carnival took place with a line-up that included singer Cleo Laine. Televised by the BBC, there were another five similar indoor events, which were the precursors of the Notting Hill Carnival.

In 2008, Claudia Jones was commemorated on a Royal Mail stamp. Like our blue plaques, our country's commemorative stamps have also represented a cross-section of society, be it a civil rights activists or poets. Dylan Thomas was one of ten remarkable people whose images were featured on postage stamps as their centenaries fell in 2014.

DYLAN THOMAS

Born in Swansea in 1914, Dylan Thomas was loved by his fellow Welsh, yet he wrote predominantly in English. His most famous works include *And Death Shall have no Dominion* and *Do Not Go Gentle Into That Good Night*, as well as his classic play *Under Milk Wood*.

In the late 1940s he found a wider audience through his BBC radio broadcasts, with *A Child's Christmas in Wales* and *Portrait of the Artist as a Young Dog* being particularly popular. He undertook four trips to the USA and, while this brought him a degree of recognition, his erratic behaviour and alcohol intake cemented his reputation as a carouser and roisterer.

The mantle of the 'doomed poet' proved to be all too real when he fell into a coma in New York while on his fourth tour of the States. He never regained consciousness.

Dylan Thomas was just 39 when he died, as was the composer Frédéric Chopin.

FRÉDÉRIC CHOPIN

Frédéric Chopin was born as Fryderyk Franciszek Szopen on 1st March, 1810, in Zelazowa Wola in Warsaw, now Poland. His mother introduced him to music as a young child, and by the age of 6 he was proficient at both playing piano and composing his own music. He quickly outpaced the music teacher his family had engaged for him and became something of a child prodigy. When he was just 16, his parents enrolled him at the Warsaw Conservatory, and he went on from there to Vienna, a city that hosted his professional debut in 1829 at the age of 19.

He delighted audiences across Europe with his expressive and technically accomplished playing. He made his home in Paris in 1832 and befriended many other now-famous composers, including Felix Mendelssohn and Franz Liszt.His relationship with the novelist Amantine Dupin, AKA George Sand, was passionate but eventually doomed. When the couple finally split in 1848, Chopin threw himself into his work and embarked on an exhaustive tour of the British Isles, which is thought to have contributed to his death a year later at 39 years of age.

GREATER LONDON COUNCIL
From this house in 1848
FREDERIC
CHOPIN
1810 - 1849
went to Guildhall to give his last public performance

Chopin's music is honoured in a modern compostion and reading called **A Prayer of William Penn**, *performed by Anton Kingsbury and Josh Verbae.*

WILLIAM PENN

William Penn was born in 1644, at Tower Hill, London. Penn's father had been knighted by Charles II for his support and help during the Restoration. In Penn's youth, their neighbour Samuel Pepys attempted, unsuccessfully, to seduce both his mother and sister. (I'm not sure if the failures were recorded in Pepys' diary). Penn was educated at Chigwell School but the family were then temporarily exiled in Ireland. It was there that William met a Quaker missionary, later admitting that 'the Lord visited me and gave me divine Impressions of Himself'.

After the death of Cromwell and the Restoration, Penn attended Christ Church, Oxford, where William Shakespeare was considered unworthy to be studied, and rather 'low-brow'. Penn and his father, also named William, had an increasingly volatile relationship and a distinct lack of understanding of each other's sensibilities.

After a spell at the court of Louis XIV, Penn decided to eschew any religious beliefs that were forced upon him and find his own theological path. Back in Cork, at the age of 22, he became a Quaker; this was much to the annoyance of his father, who insisted that his son left home and that he would be disinherited.

Quakers were treated as heretics by the Crown, and Penn's first pamphlet criticising all other religious groups, *Truth Exalted To Princes, Priests and People*, was criticized by Pepys. It may, of course, have been sour grapes due to his unsuccessful seduction attempts, as he wrote it off as a 'ridiculous nonsensical book', that he was 'ashamed to read.'

Penn, a champion of democracy and religious freedom, was imprisoned in the Tower of London following his second pamphlet, *The Sandy Foundation Shaken*. During his eight month solitary incarceration he wrote a second treatise rather than recant the first. Whilst in gaol he also wrote the book that would become a Christian classic, *No Cross, No Crown*. He was later sent to Newgate having been exonerated by a jury, who the judge also sent to jail, basically for disagreeing with him. Fighting their case from prison, the jury won the right for all English juries to be free from the absolute control of judges, and it proved to be a victory for the use of the writ of habeas corpus.

Penn's father eventually came to admire his son for his beliefs and didn't disinherit him, although Penn did return to jail again for six months for his persistent views.

In 1681, Charles II gave William Penn senior a substantial piece of land in America, to appease a debt he owed him. This passed to his son, and Penn set sail from England to the land which is present day Pennsylvania and Delaware, landing at New Castle in 1682, and receiving a pledge of allegiance from his fellow colonists. Penn later founded Philadelphia, but all was not well in what is now Delaware; the Swedish, Dutch and English settlers weren't overly enthusiastic about Penn's Quaker government. Petitioning for their own assembly, the three southernmost counties of Pennsylvania split, to become the colony of Lower Delaware. Penn's negotiating skills and diplomacy led to good relations and successful treaties with the Lenape Native Americans.

Penn pushed for a union of the English colonies, which would eventually come about as the United States of America. The democratic principles in his Pennsylvania Frame of Government would inspire the United States Constitution. His futuristic ideas led him to develop a project for a United States of Europe and the creation of a European Parliament.

Penn married twice, the second time to 25-year-old Hannah Callowhill, when he was 52. Both marriages resulted in eight children each. In 1984, US President Ronald Reagan would declare William Penn and Hannah Callowhill-Penn to be Honorary Citizens of the United States. Penn returned to England in 1701, having poured money into America for little return. Back home he wrestled with financial problems, including his son William's colossal gambling debts and the fact that his financial advisor had cheated him out of thousands of pounds. He unsuccessfully tried to sell Pennsyvania to the Crown, but by the age of 62 he found himself back in jail. Penn died penniless at Ruscombe, near Twyford in Berkshire in 1718.

Charles II giving Penn's father the land in America was the catalyst to the latter pushing for what would become the United States.

CHARLES II

Charles II was born in 1630, the son of Charles I and Henrietta Marie, the sister of Louis XIII of France. He became Prince of Wales at the age of eight and accompanied his father during the Battle of Edgehill, the first conflict of the English Civil War. With Cromwell's forces gathering momentum, Charles feared for his son's safety and sent him to France, where his cousin, the eight-year-old Louis XIV, was now the reiging monarch.

The Prince later moved on to the Hague where he had an affair with Lucy Walter and sired the first of many illegitimate children. Charles I was beheaded in January 1649 and England became a Republic. Charles signed an agreement with the Scots authorising Presbyterian church governance across Britian in exchange for their support against Cromwell.

Unsurprisingly, it won him a degree of support in Scotland,

but devalued his popularity in England. Crowned King of Scotland, he moved south with an army of men to engage the Parliamentarians, the two armies meeting at Worcester in September 1851. The heart soon went out of Charles's supporters and he was lucky to escape, and to find friends to assist him. For two weeks he avoided capture, through disguise, the shaving of his head and the cunning of his confidantes.

Eventually he engaged a boat at Shoreham and fled abroad. The atmosphere and tension of his escape is realistically and thrillingly captured in Charles Spencer's book *To Catch A King*.

There was some hope of a British expedition in 1658, but Oliver Cromwell died that year and his son Richard took over as Lord Protector. Richard however was no leader, and after the first general election for twenty years a House of Commons was formed. The Commonwealth had proved to be no better for the country than life under Charles I, so in 1660 Parliament invited Charles II to return and to take the throne. This meant him co-operating with Parliament and exercising tolerance and lenience.

BARN OF UPPER HOUSE

KING CHARLES II
HID IN
THIS BARN
5TH SEPTEMBER 1651

9

TELFORD HISTORIC BUILDING

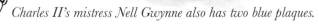

Charles II's mistress Nell Gwynne also has two blue plaques.

NELL GWYNNE

London, Oxford, and Hereford all claim to be the birthplace of Nell Gwynne, but possibly Hereford has the best claim as her grandfather, who went on to become Canon of Christ Church Oxford, was believed to have been a churchman there. As a child, though, Eleanor 'Nell' Gwynne grew up in Coal Yard Alley, near Drury Lane, and as a child worked depending on varying accounts as a bawdyhouse servant, street hawker and cinder-girl.

There are various allusions as to her having been born to a higher class family but there is nothing to substantiate the fact, nor contradict it. Her mother, who ran a bawdy house, was drowned in a pond at Chelsea, probably while drunk, in July 1679. It's almost certain that Nell worked as a child prostitute, taking a lover at the age of 12 who helped her secure a job at a theatre near Maypole Alley.

With the Restoration, Charles II legalised acting as a profession for women, and acting, especially of the comedic variety was something at which Nell Gwynne excelled. In 1663, The Kings Company opened the theatre in Bridges Street (later rebuilt as the Theatre Royal) where Nell had a job selling oranges to the clientele.

At the age of 14, less than a year after becoming an orange seller, Nell proved herself good enough to become an actress, making her stage debut in 1665. She became the mistress of Charles Hart, one of the period's leading actors, which ensured her continued success in the theatre.

The diarist, Samuel Pepys, reported himself delighted by the performance of 'pretty, witty Nell', watching her as Florimel in Dryden's Secret Love, or the Maiden Queen.

He wrote: 'so great a performance of a comical part was never, I believe, in the world before… so done by Nell her merry part as cannot be better done in nature', Dryden later wrote plays specifically to exploit her talents as a comic actress. Nell was extremely pretty, with long reddish-brown hair and a good figure, reckless but generous and unpretentious. She was known to be illiterate and could only sign her name with her awkwardly scrawled initials 'E.G.'.

She remained a member of the Drury Lane acting company until 1669, playing continuously except for a short period in Epsom in the summer of 1667, when she lived as the mistress of Charles Sackville, styled Lord Buckhurst and later 6th Earl of Dorset, Sackville paying her so she didn't have to rely on acting.

She was soon back on the stage, with the 2nd Duke of Buckingham, George Villiers attempting to set her up as the King's mistress; her demand of £500 was rejected as being too expensive. She did become his mistress though, after Charles flirted with her at the theatre and invited her to supper.

He is alleged to have discovered that he had no money with him and asked Nell to foot the bill. Her supposed response was an impression of the King, exclaiming, 'Od's fish... but this is the poorest company I ever was in'.

Having previously been the mistress of Charles Hart and Charles Sackville, she jokingly referred to the King as her 'Charles the Third.' Nell's acting career ended at the age of twenty-one. She had borne the King a son in Charles Beauclerk, who became the Earl of Burford and later the First Duke of St Albans. In 1671 she moved into a townhouse at 79, Pall Mall, for which she was given the freehold, and gave birth to a second son, James Beauclerk.

Nell died in 1687 at her house in Pall Mall.

Samantha Cameron, the wife of former Prime Minister David Cameron, is Nell Gwynne's great-great-great-great-great-great-great granddaughter, and her great-grandmother, Enid Bagnold, also has a blue plaque.

ENID BAGNOLD

Born in Rochester, Kent in 1889, Bagnold was mainly raised in Jamaica, but attended art school in London and went on to work for the London-based writer and publisher, Frank Harris. She worked as a nurse during WWI and later became a driver in France until the end of the conflict.

She wrote about her nursing experience in *A Diary Without Dates* and her time as a driver in *The Happy Foreigner*. In 1920, she married Sir Roderick Jones, the chairman of Reuters. The couple moved to North End House, the former home of Edward Burne-Jones near Brighton, at Rottingdean. Her book *National Velvet* was published in 1935, with a film version starring Mickey Rooney and Elizabeth Taylor following in 1944.

In 2003, the movie of *National Velvet* was selected for preservation in the United States National Film Registry by the Library of Congress as being 'culturally, historically, or aesthetically significant.' The garden of their house on the south coast inspired her play *The Chalk Garden* which premiered on Broadway in 1955 and starred Ethel Barrymore, with sets and costumes by Cecil Beaton.

The British premiere, at the Theatre Royal, Haymarket the following year, was directed by John Gielgud and starred Edith Evans and Peggy Ashcroft.

Enid Bagnold died at Rottingdean in 1981.

ENGLISH HERITAGE
ENID
BAGNOLD
1889~1981
Novelist
and
Playwright
lived here

Bagnold had served as a nurse during WW1. So, rather more famously, had our next subject Edith Cavell.

EDITH CAVELL

Edith Louisa Cavell was born in 1865. She trained at The London Hospital, working 14 hour days for a salary of £10 a year. During WWI she saved lives on both sides, as well as helping some 200 Allied soldiers escape from Belgium, then occupied by Germany.

She was arrested, accused of treason, found guilty by court-martial and sentenced to death. International pleas for clemency fell on deaf ears and she was shot by a German firing squad.

Laurence Binyon wrote a poem about her that begins;
She was binding the wounds of her enemies when they came—
The lint in her hand unrolled.
They battered the door with their rifle-butts, crashed
it in:
She faced them gentle and bold.

And ends:

The hurts she healed, the
thousands comforted—these

Make a fragrance of her
fame.

But because she stept to
her star right on through
death

It is Victory speaks her name.

---

 *Her memorial service, in October 1915 at St Paul's, included **Abide With Me**, the hymn said to be on her lips as she was executed. It was written by Henry Francis Lyte.*

HENRY FRANCIS LYTE

Henry Francis Lyte wrote *Abide With Me* at Berry Head House, Brixham in 1847, the year that fellow plaque recipient Charlotte Brontë's *Jane Eyre* was published, and also the year that another plaque awardee, Annie Besant was born.

Lyte was born in Kelso, Scotland and educated at Portora Royal School in Einiskillen, County Fermanagh (which now has a commemorative plaque), and was effectively adopted by the headmaster after Lyte's mother and brother died.

He studied at Trinity College, Dublin and had an evangelical conversion in around 1816. Lyte looked after several parishes before becoming the curate of Marazion in Cornwall and marrying Scottish Methodist Anne Maxwell the following year.

Lyte also enjoyed archaeology, playing the flute, was an avid bibliophile, and a fierce opponent of slavery.

Plagued in later years by tuberculosis, asthma and bronchitis, he died a couple of months after composing *Abide With Me*, the hymn that would become a favourite of George V and George VI.

Abide With Me *has been sung at the FA Cup Final since the Arsenal v Cardiff match in 1927, after the Association's secretary substituted it instead of playing Alexander's Ragtime Band. Since 1929 it has also been sung at the Rugby League Challenge Cup Final.*

THE FOOTBALL ASSOCIATION

The 150th Anniversary of the Football Association was marked with a blue plaque at Wembley in 2013.

The occasion was marked by the FA inviting 16 descendants of the eight men who drafted football's original 13 laws. Isaac Lord, seven, the youngest of George Twizell Wawn's descendants, was given the honour of unveiling a plaque commemorating the founders with former England International, Sir Trevor Brooking CBE.

The Laws of Association Football were first drawn up by Ebenezer Cobb Morley (left)and approved at a meeting of the newly founded Football Association on 8 December 1863, and although he had no descendants, the FA discovered relatives of the other eight men as far afield as Washington DC, Chicago and Auckland, and flew them to Wembley for the unveiling.

Alex Horne, General Secretary of The FA, believes the achievements of the Founding Fathers can now be properly celebrated:

'In terms of historical significance, the eight Founding Fathers of football should be placed alongside other great pioneers of this nation. The FA is delighted that in its 150th year we have been able to identify living descendants and honour their forefathers at what is now the home of English football, Wembley.'

As we've just celebrated the FA's 150th anniversary, let's have a quick glance at a few of the initial established rules of the game:

'The goal shall be defined by two upright posts without any tape or bar across them. No player shall run with the ball. Neither tripping nor hacking shall be allowed, and no player shall use his hands to hold or push his adversary.

A player shall not be allowed to throw the ball or pass it to another with his hands. No player shall be allowed to take the ball from the ground with his hands under any pretence whatever while it is in play. No player shall be allowed to wear projecting nails, iron plates on the soles or heels of his boots.'

.

Commemorating
the
Founding Fathers of football
to mark the
150th anniversary of
The Football Association
Formed
26 October 1863

British Plaque Trust

Which leads us to English football's finest hour; winning the World Cup at Wembley in 1966. The team captain, of course, was Bobby Moore.

BOBBY MOORE

The Captain of England's World Cup-winning side was Bobby Moore, born in Barking in 1941. He played school football before joining West Ham United in 1956; his debut first team match came two years later against Manchester United. Moore was called up for the England Under 23 squad in 1960, earning his first full England cap in 1962. He was elevated to captain on just his 12th appearance for his country, after Johnny Haynes retired.

He skippered West Ham United to win the FA Cup in 1964, was named Football Writers' Association Footballer of the Year, and became the regular choice as England Captain. A year later he steered West Ham to victory in the European Cup Winners Cup, and in 1966 led England to their World Cup victory, beating West Germany 4-2 in the final to lift the Jules Rimet Trophy.

Following the win, Moore won the BBC Sports Personality of the Year and was awarded the OBE. He also captained the England side during the Mexico World Cup. In 1973, he won his 108th and final International cap, and made his 90th appearance as England captain, equalling Billy Wright's tally. They still jointly hold the record. In 1874 he joined Fulham, before moving on to play his final soccer in North America before retiring in 1978. In the early 1990s he worked as a commentator for the London Radio Station Capital Gold, making his last appearance in 1993, just a week before his untimely death from cancer.

His memorial service was held at Westminster Abbey, only the second sportsman to be so honoured, with the rest of the World Cup squad in attendance. In 2002 Bobby Moore was made an inaugural inductee of the English Football Hall of Fame, the same year being named in the BBC's list of 100 Greatest Britons.

In 2003 Prince Andrew unveiled the World Cup Sculpture near West Ham's Boleyn Ground, depicting Moore holding the Jules Rimet Cup aloft. Four years later a statue of Moore was unveiled by Sir Bobby Charlton at Wembley Stadium. On 26th July 2016 he was honoured with a blue plaque at his childhood home in Waverley Gardens, Barking, with his daughter Roberta in attendance. England Manager Alf Ramsay paid tribute to Bobby Moore:

'My captain, my leader, my right-hand man. He was the spirit and the heartbeat of the team. A cool, calculating footballer I could trust with my life. He was the supreme professional, the best I ever worked with. Without him England would never have won the World Cup.'

Bobby Moore's plaque was one of several unveiled for the 150th anniversary of the conception of the blue plaques scheme. Another was for Thomas Barnardo, the founder of Barnardo's Homes.

THOMAS BARNARDO

Born in Dublin in 1845, Thomas Barnardo left for London at the age of seventeen to train as a doctor at the London Hospital in Whitechapel, with a view to becoming a medical missionary in China.

Soon after his arrival, an outbreak of cholera swept through London's East End, killing more than 3,000 people. Many families were left destitute and sleeping rough, with thousands of children begging on the streets. He was so moved that he gave up on the idea of going to China and decided to devote his energies to helping destitute and impoverished children.

In 1870, he opened his first home for boys in Stepney, teaching them carpentry, metalwork and shoemaking. He initially limited the number of boys, but after the death of an 11-year-old boy, John Somers, from malnutrition and exposure, who'd been turned away because the shelter was full, he vowed never turn away another child.

His motto became 'No destitute child ever refused admission'. In just seven years, Barnardo established a ragged school, a children's home and employment agency, and a mission church, also buying up a children's magazine.

After his marriage to fellow evangelist and philanthropist, Syrie Louise Elmslie, they took a 15-year lease on Mossford Lodge in Barkingside and opened a home for girls. By 1900, the development included 65 cottages, a school, a hospital, and a church, built around three village greens, and within twenty years would be able to house 1,500 girls, most of whom were trained for such work as domestic service, with some being trained as nursery nurses.

By the time Barnardo died in 1905 his charity had opened 96 homes caring for more than 8,500 children.

Another blue plaque recipient who was similarly concerned with the welfare of the less fortunate and those in straitened circumstances was Octavia Hill.

OCTAVIA HILL

Octavia Hill was born in 1838. She began helping working people when she was just fourteen, making toys for children from the Ragged School.

She became a major force behind the development of social housing, with John Ruskin backing her financially. She made a point of getting to know the tenants personally, encouraging them to better themselves. In her opinion, 'municipal socialism and subsidised housing' led to indiscriminate demolition, re-housing schemes and the destruction of communities.

Hill was also concerned about the lack of open spaces for people in crowded slums and tenements, campaigning vehemently against the development of existing woodland, and helping to save Hampstead Heath and Parliament Hill Fields.

She said 'I think we want four things. Places to sit in, places to play in, places to stroll in and places to spend a day in.' To this end, she was one of the three founders of the National Trust, set up to preserve places of historic interest or natural beauty. Mooted in 1893 by Hill, the Canon Hardwicke Ranwsley, and Sir Robert Hunter, they rejected the name the Commons and Gardens Trust and went for The National Trust.

Hill coined the phrase 'green belt', and wasa lso a founder member of the Charity Organisation Society, now the charity Family Action, and a member of the Royal Commission on the Poor Laws. She also created the Southwark detachment of the Army Cadet Force, its first independent unit.

In a speech in 1898 she said: 'When I am gone, I hope my friends will not try to carry out any special system, or to follow blindly in the track which I have trodden. New circumstances require various efforts, and it is the spirit, not the dead form, that should perpetuated.'

She is commemorated with a monument on the hill at Hydon Ball in Surrey. Her birthplace in Wisbech has been turned into the Octavia Hill Museum, and the Octavia Hill Society was set up in 1992 'to promote awareness of the ideas and ideals of Octavia Hill, her family, fellow workers and their relevance in today's society nationally and internationally.'

The National Trust that Octavia Hill founded now maintains and protects many hundreds of sites and properties across the UK. One of them is the John F. Kennedy Memorial at Runnymede.

JOHN F. KENNEDY

John Fitzgerald Kennedy was born in Massachusetts in 1917. He became the 35th President of the United States of America in January 1961, and was sadly assassinated in the November of 1963, in Dallas, Texas.

Kennedy has a blue plaque at Princes Gate, London as his father Joe was based there as United States Ambassador to the Court of St. James from 1938-1940.

During this period, John and his sister, Kathleen 'Kick' Kennedy, enjoyed the nightlife of London and hanging out with the young society set doing the rounds of the nightclubs, a favourite being the 400 Club in Leicester Square.

Joe Kennedy fell out with Winston Churchill after supporting a policy of appeasement with Hitler, seeking a meeting with him, without the approval of the US. Department of State, in order 'to bring about a better understanding between Germany and the United States.' He also argued against the US providing military and economic aid to Britain, stating, 'Democracy is finished in England'.

British MP Josiah Wedgewood, 1st Baron Wedgewood, said of Joe Kennedy, 'We have a rich man, untrained in diplomacy, unlearned in history and politics, who is a great publicity seeker and who apparently is ambitious to be the first Catholic president of the US.'

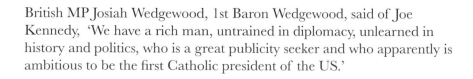

While the Royal Family, the Prime Minister, government ministers and other ambassadors stayed in London during the Blitz, Kennedy retreated to the country and was later recalled to the States by Roosevelt as he was clearly out of step with Roosevelt's policies.

In London, the young JFK wasn't short of girlfriends, and reportedly had just had a fling with with Marlene Dietrich on the French Riviera. After meeting the young Princess Elizabeth with King George VI and the Queen, he even cheekily wrote to a friend that 'I think she rather liked me, and now I wouldn't be surprised if she had a thing for me.'

The Kennedy's former residence in Prince's Gate was built in the 1840s and recently sold for £70 million.

JOHN
FITZGERALD
KENNEDY
PRESIDENT
UNITED STATES OF
AMERICA
1961 – 1963
LIVED HERE

◆

Like his father Joe, JFK attended Harvard, the prestigious American University named after John Harvard in Cambridge, Massachusetts. He wrote in his application that 'to be a "Harvard man" is an enviable distinction, and one that I sincerely hope I shall attain.'

JOHN HARVARD

John Harvard was born in 1607 in Southwark, then in the county of Surrey, the fourth of nine children born to butcher and tavern owner, Robert Harvard. John attended St. Saviour's Grammar School, but in 1625 the bubonic plague reduced the family to John, his brother Thomas and their mother, Katherine. Having been left some property, John's mother was able to send him to Emmanuel College, Cambridge where he earned his BA in 1632, his MA in 1635, and was ordained dissenting minister.

The following year he married Ann Sadler of Ringmer, the couple emigrating to New England in 1637, where Harvard became a freeman of Massachusetts. They settled in Charlestown, bought some land, built a house, and John became an assistant preacher. Harvard died from tuberculosis at the age of thirty and was buried at Charlestown.

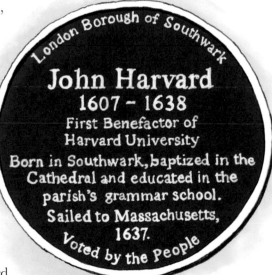

His deathbed bequest to the college founded by the Massachusetts Bay Colony two years earlier was so gratefully received that it was ordered 'that the Colledge agreed upon formerly to bee built at Cambridg sjalbee called Harvard Colledge.'

John Harvard's grandfather, Thomas Rogers, had been an associate of William Shakespeare, both serving on the borough corporation's council.

WILLIAM SHAKESPEARE

'Remember me', Hamlet said; words given to him by the most famous, celebrated, and famous writer in the world. What better way to sum up the important role of blue plaques? And what better way to round off this book than with William Shakespeare himself.

Shakespeare's personal life is somewhat mysterious, and various rumours and claims about his biographical details, and even the true authorship of some of his most famous works, continue to this day.

We do know that he was born in April 1564 in Stratford-Upon-Avon, to John Shakespeare, a successful merchant in leather goods and and Mary Arden. He was the third child, having two older sisters, Joan and Judith, and three younger brothers, Richard, Gilbert, and Edmund.

Little is known about Shakespeare's childhood and education; it's assumed that he was educated at the local King's New School in Stratford, but we can't know for certain as no official records exist. There are a total of seven years where no information exists about Shakespeare's life at all, so much of his biography is conjecture. Shakespeare was married to Anne Hathaway, eight years his senior at 26, in Worcester on 28th November 1582. Hathaway was pregnant with their first child Susanna, and the couple also produced twins, Hamnet and Judith, two years after.

Shakespeare became an actor, playing with (and partner in) the popular company The Chamberlain's Men, later The King's Men, after the coronation of James I. Shakespeare's earliest known works were written and published at this time. Despite the theatre being frowned upon by much of the establishment, Shakespeare became successful and patronised by several aristocrats, establishing The Globe Theatre with his partners in 1599. He became quite well off, investing his money wisely, and it's thought that this financial security gave him the independence to write and develop his own plays.

His name is now known around the world, mainly for his 37 plays and possibly less so for his 154 sonnets, and he's widely considered to be our greatest writer and playwright. In a BBC poll in 1999, Shakespeare was voted 'British Personality of the Millennium.

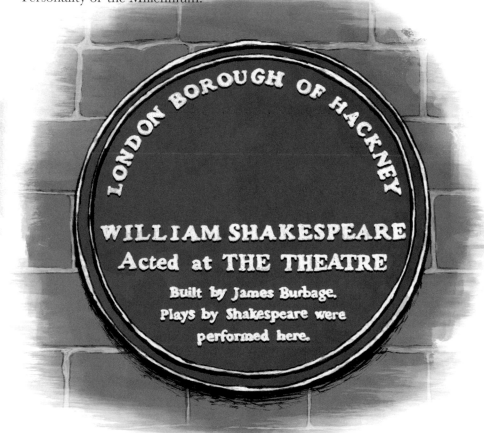

'Praising what is lost makes the remembrance dear'.
- *William Shakespeare*

ABOUT THE AUTHOR

Mike Read is a bestselling author and presenter.

He has had thirty-six books published; these include his autobiography *Seize the Day*, *Forever England*, a biography of Rupert Brooke, and *1,000 Years of Caversham Park*. He topped the Sunday Times bestseller list with *The Guinness Book of Hit Singles*, and was also given a Guinness sales award.

He was created a Knight of Malta in 2011, and founded the Rupert Brooke Society and Museum in 1999. He is Chairman of the British Plaque Trust and was heavily involved in the creation of the 50 blue plaques to music icons for BBC Music Day in 2017. Mike is also an Ambassador for the Prince's Trust and was Chairman of the Lords and Commons Entertainment Committee for several years. He has twice been asked to stand as London Mayor.

Mike Read has won ten National Broadcaster of the Year Awards, an International Music award, and has been awarded the Gold Badge of Merit by the Music Association for his special contribution to Britain's music industry. A household name in Britain for 40 years having fronted three top-rated long-running TV series, *Top of the Pops*, *Pop Quiz* & *Saturday Superstore* and three national radio breakfast shows, including Radio One and Classic FM.

He features every few weeks on the repeats of *Top of the Pops* on BBC Four and presented two *Pop Quiz* specials for the BBC in 2016/2017. 2016 saw him continuing to present programmes for the BBC as well as producing and presenting a new TV series, *Tin Pan Alley*, which ran for 8 weeks on Sky in 2016. A global distributor is now selling the format to territories around the world.

During 2016 and 2017 he wrote and filmed a six part series, *Jamaicaphiles*, working with the Jamaican Tourist Board, which featured Noël Coward, Oscar Hammerstein, Ian Fleming, Errol Flynn, John F. Kennedy and Johnny Cash.

Mike has written several film scripts, had had eight musicals staged and has penned songs for over forty major artists including Cliff Richard, The Bee Gees, Marc Almond, Boy George, Gene Pitney, Don McLean, Brian Wilson, Barry & Robin Gibb, Donovan, David Essex, Steve Harley, Steve Winwood, Justin Hayward and many others.

Mike has had several chart hits, has twice topped the Independent singles chart and recently had a bestselling CD featuring his settings of Rupert Brooke's War Sonnets, featuring the Kings College Choir & the Eton College Chapel Choir.

He regularly travels to different parts of the world broadcasting or giving talks, including, Russia, Estonia, Australia, the USA, Malta, Jamaica, Mexico, Nicaragua, Hawaii, Honolulu, Norway, Denmark, Finland, Sweden, France, Spain, Portugal, South Africa, Turkey, The Canary Islands, Greece, Croatia, Italy, the Canary Islands, the Azores and many of the Caribbean Islands.

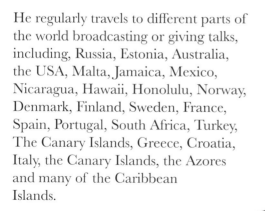

ACKNOWLEDGEMENTS

―――――――◆―――――――

Our industrious historians at the British Plaque Trust, Ian Freeman, Nicky Cox, Charles 9th Earl Spencer, and Lord Grade. James Stewart and his team at the BBC for all their hard work and professionalism in helping to make the 2017 BBC Music Day Plaques such a success. The team at Unicorn, and the Commonwealth Society for their encouragement in extending our scheme across the Commonwealth; and of course, all the incredible people who have proved themselves worthy of a blue plaque and made a special contribution to our country.

―――――――◆―――――――